Raising a Mensch

Raising a Mensch

Shelley Kapnek Rosenberg, Ed.D.

• • • • • • • • • • • • •

2003 • 5763
The Jewish Publication Society
Philadelphia

The Jewish Publication Society
2100 Arch Street, 2nd floor
Philadelphia, PA 19103

Design and Composition by Sasgen Graphic Design

Manufactured in the United States of America
03 04 05 06 07 08 09 10 11 12   10 9 8 7 6 5 4 3 2 1

Library of Congress Cataloging-in-Publication Data
Rosenberg, Shelly Kapnek
  Raising a mensch /Shelley Kapnek Rosenberg.— 1st ed.
    p.cm.
  Includes bibliographical references and index.
  ISBN 0-8276-0754-7
  1. Moral development. 2. Parent and child. 3. child rearing. 4. Ethics,
Jewish. I. Title.
  BF723.M54 R68 2003
  296.7'4—dc21

                    20021544016

The publication of this book
was made possible by a gift from

Arabelle and Lewis Kapnek

and is lovingly dedicated to our parents,
children, and grandchildren.

To my parents, Arabelle and Lewis Kapnek,
and to my husband, Kenneth,
my exemplars of menschlichkeit

And to Michael and Jessica Rosenberg:
"So follow the way of the good
And keep to the paths of the just.
For the upright will inhabit the earth . . .
—Proverbs 2:20–21

Contents

Acknowledgments

When Ellen Frankel, editor-in-chief of The Jewish Publication Society, suggested that I write a book on improving children's moral lives, I was flattered—and terrified. Although I have been an educator for more than thirty years and a parent for more than twenty-two, I wondered exactly what I would be able to tell other parents about a subject so delicate and strewn with mines.

I began interviewing rabbis, psychologists, psychiatrists, social workers, and other educators. I hoped that they would tell me something brilliant, something I didn't know, something that I would then quote to help parents dispel the mystery of raising *menschlich* kids. After eight months of interviews, of trying to learn what other people knew, I learned how much I knew. And Ellen Frankel told me to trust myself and allow myself to be the expert. I thank Ellen for the initial opportunity to write this book and, even more, for the vote of confidence.

As I worked, there were a number of people who were willing to read the manuscript while it remained a work in process, offer excellent advice, answer questions, and generally serve as a sounding board for my ideas. I wish to thank Helene Z. Tigay, Sharon Charish, Rabbi

Richard Fagan, Nancy Messinger, Dr. Elizabeth Berger, Dr. Carol Ingall, Dr. Joel Schwartz, and Thomas "Woody" Price.

I sincerely believe that a good writer is that much better when working with a good editor. Many thanks are owed to Carol Hupping, JPS publishing director, and Kristina Espy, Editorial Assistant, and Candace Levy, copyeditor, for the painstaking care that helped me say what I wanted to say in the clearest possible way.

Writing a book is somewhat like giving birth—only it takes longer! It is a tremendous commitment of time, energy, and emotion. The reason that I have now been able to complete two books (and can think seriously about starting a third) is the incredible support I receive daily from my family. My parents, Arabelle and Lewis Kapnek, have always told me that I could accomplish anything and everything I wanted. They have been my most loyal cheerleaders from the very beginning. My in-laws, Roslyn and Lester Cohen, and my sister, sisters-in-law, and brothers-in-law, Hilary and Todd Alexander, Carol and Stuart Fisher, and Rich and Ann Rosenberg, have been there for me, too, patiently listening to my ideas and concerns and offering loving encouragement.

And, of course, my two miracles—Michael and Jessica—and my dearest friend and partner, my husband, Ken, have given me the greatest gifts of all—the will and reason to write this book, their unfailing love, and the good humor to overlook my lack of interest in things domestic when I'm busy writing. I love them more than words can express.

To all of you—heartfelt and enduring thanks. 🌾

Introduction

"Kids! What's the matter with kids today?" So goes the chorus of a song from a famous 1950s musical. Back then parents worried about dating behavior, the negative influence of the latest heartthrob musician, and the fact that their children routinely ignored their well-meaning advice. Today's parents might sing the same refrain, but the verses might be lamenting aggression and violence, dishonesty, drug and alcohol abuse, sexually transmitted diseases, teen pregnancy, and their children's general lack of a moral compass.

Yet we might also ask, "Parents! What's the matter with parents today?" In studies on the moral climate existing among children nowadays, kids report that they don't receive clear, consistent messages about moral behavior from home, school, or community. Moreover, their experience is that ethical violations are largely ignored or tolerated. Some parents seem to care more about the outcome than how their children arrive there. Others lack the will to contend with their children's unacceptable behavior. If this is the case, then we have failed our children dramatically. For it is primarily from us, their parents, that children learn what ethical behavior is, that it matters, that the end doesn't justify the means, and that how they make the journey is as important as the destination.

What Jewish parents have discovered, much to our chagrin, is that we are not exempt from the problems plaguing parents in general. The maxims "good Jewish boys don't . . ." or "nice Jewish girls wouldn't . . ." not only don't apply but are outdated. We no longer live, work, study, and play entirely within the protective cocoon of our Jewish community, untouched by the world, influenced only by our own values, responsible only to our own mores and rules. Breaking out of this cocoon may have provided an added measure of freedom, but it has left many of us feeling a bit adrift, lacking the support of the community that buttressed prior generations. Moreover, we live in what Rabbi Nancy Fuchs Kramer, author of *Parenting as a Spiritual Journey,* calls "a kid-unfriendly culture, driven by money and advertising, that is toxic to developing values." Our children are involved in and influenced by American society and culture—for good as well as for ill.

This seems also to be a time of shifting moral values. There are more pros and cons to consider and more complex decisions to make. Society's rules don't seem so hard and fast, right and wrong don't seem so absolute. And technology, with all its benefits, has in some ways removed us from our neighbors. When we no longer see the face or know the name of someone we might hurt, poor behavior somehow doesn't seem so bad.

Some of us may not have carefully thought out and articulated our own moral standards, making it even more difficult to convey what we believe to our children. Some of us doubt and second-guess ourselves; we may have difficulty squaring our youthful indiscretions with what we desire of our kids. And some of us wish to be "friends" with our children instead of accepting our position as role models and exemplars of what we Jews call menschlich (fully human) behavior.

We are right to be concerned. It is our responsibility as parents—as our children's first and, we hope, best teachers—to work for change. Can we improve our children's moral lives? We can and we must.

The good news is that help is available. Jewish parents of all manner of belief and ritual observance need look no farther than their own tradition. Thousands of years of accumulated wisdom, starting with the ten most basic of premises, expand to encompass a complete code of virtuous behavior. Judaism offers us the tools, if we choose to use them, to improve our own moral lives—and our children's.

THE WORLD'S MOST CHALLENGING JOB

Parents stumble into what is arguably the most challenging job in the world with little, if any, preparation. Few of us would even consider applying for a professional position for which we had no formal training, no classes, no practicum, and no internship. Yet we undertake parenting—a complex combination of teaching, coaching, doctoring, counseling, cheerleading, and lawyering—with little more than a hope and a prayer.

We had an "observership" long ago, as our parents practiced their parenting skills, which were equally untrained and perhaps as limited, on us. If we were lucky, our parents were loving, kind, and nurturing; they were role models for good parenting. Some of us, however, were not so lucky. Some of us experienced abuse, violence, and neglect or had parents who were dealing with drug addiction, alcoholism, or workaholism. And even the vast majority of us, who are from caring, supportive homes, were unlikely to have had many instructive discussions about ethics and morality with our parents. It would never have occurred to that generation to engage us in that way. For good or bad, our parenting skills were shaped in the laboratory of our family of origin.

The issues that our children and we confront in this day and age seem especially complex. Our children face all of the same challenges we did, and more. The ready availability and affordability of alcohol and designer drugs can easily lead to abuse. Premarital sex is now linked not only with pregnancy but also with sexually transmitted diseases that kill. Violence on television, in the movies, and in video games may blunt children's reactions to the horror of injuring another human being. Weapons show up in schools and on playgrounds and in the hands of youngsters who are hurt and angry at being taunted, bullied, and victimized because they don't wear the right clothes or belong to the cool group. Popular kids are themselves worried and unsure, victimizing others to enhance their own shaky self-esteem. Insecurities about body image become potentially fatal eating disorders. Intense pressure to make good grades and win admission to top-ranked colleges encourages the cheating that is rife in our schools. We live in a culture of ruthlessness that seems to reward success at any price. And we often feel too far removed from one another to offer consolation and caring.

Many parents feel adrift in unfamiliar territory with no roadmap or guide. Few of us have had to think long or hard about our personal moral code, let alone declare it coherently to others. We are not certain of exactly what we want to say or how to say it. Articulating one's values is even more difficult when talking to children, who have a vocabulary and an agenda all their own. It is especially challenging when the children are our own, since our dearest hope is that they accept what we offer.

Some of us want to be popular—liked as well as loved by our kids—and so we have even greater difficulty taking a stand, knowing that by doing so we risk having our children reject not only what we tell them but us as well. But good parenting sometimes involves telling kids hard truths, things they won't like. It means making tough decisions, facing our children's displeasure and even their anger, knowing that what we are doing needs to be done.

At the same time, parents want to address the big issues. We should be selective, carefully choosing the issues that we want to stress. We must recognize that our kids will turn us off if everything is a big issue. And we must gradually allow them increasing amounts of space and the opportunities to make their own decisions. At a certain point, our children will continue to build their own moral codes, based on the foundation that we have provided.

Some parents do not even recognize that they, and their children, are adrift. They see the problems that they read about in the morning paper or hear about on the evening news as somebody else's problems. They are in denial, believing that they are exempt from and untouched by the issues that confront the rest of us. They respond to a teacher's phone call with an angry "Not my child!" or appear with their lawyers, ready to bail their children out of trouble. Even though their children's behavior shocks and dismays, these parents are adamant that there are no problems.

THE PRESSURES MOUNT

Outside influences and pressures add to a parent's challenge. Time is fleeting. The hours of each day often move by too quickly, and when gone they can never be recovered. In the hustle and bustle of our busy world, parenting becomes the work we do after the "real" work—the tasks that bring home a paycheck—of our day. The old saw about quality of time compensating for a lack of quantity of time is really just that—an old saw. The rushed minutes and hurried half hours fit in between work and the other demands of a busy schedule can compromise the quality of that time. We are often, as Barbara Coloroso, author of *Kids Are Worth It,* says, "not really present to our children," even when we are with them. If we are mulling over the phone call from our most important client or are mentally preparing tomorrow's presentation, we are not thinking clearly about our child's dilemma with the class bully. We are not focusing on our child, and he or she knows it. Our physical presence is, in such cases, limited in value.

The messages that bombard us and our children from our technologically advanced, very competitive world don't support virtue; they belittle it. And far too many parents accept these messages. Ask some parents what constitutes success or what they hope their children will be when they grow up. Danny Siegel, the "Mitzvah Man," author of *Heroes and Miracle Workers, Mitzvahs,* and countless other books on *mitzvot,* does this all the time. Most parents, he reports, talk about financial and material success. They talk about "a good college, leading to a good job, leading to earning a good salary." Precious few, if any, talk about their children becoming happy people, good people, or giving people. What, then, can these parents be teaching their children about what is important in life?

Today, it is easy for such messages about success to infiltrate Jewish families, as many of us do not have support from our extended families and communities. In the not-so-distant past, multiple generations lived together, or in close proximity, so children learned not only from parents but also from grandparents, aunts, uncles, and cousins. The synagogue was central to Jewish existence, and the community was a constant presence, where members felt free to offer advice about every aspect of life. In the shtetl, raising children was a group project, and the community's values were the norm. The Jewish community was the village that raised its children. Everyone knew everyone and knew everyone's business. If your own mother wasn't watching, you could be sure that the *bubbe* next door was—whether or not she really was your *bubbe*.

In the twenty-first century, families are spread around the country and even around the globe. Children often have little sense of their family's mores, customs, and traditions. Some visit grandparents and other extended family only once or twice a year. Neighborhoods are no longer neighborly, and the synagogue, if a family is affiliated, may not be in the immediate neighborhood. The synagogue may be just one more stop for the afternoon carpool, between Little League and piano lessons. It is difficult to feel that we belong to anything and that anything really belongs to us. While we are free from the tyranny of the community, we also lack its support. Often, all we know of what the community thinks is from listening to our children's plaintive cry that "Everybody else is doing it."

Yet family and communal support can be critical to parents who are struggling to define their own values and convey them to their children. Whether we are aware of it or not, our children are constantly watching us and the other adults in their lives. Role models all, we must always consider what our children learn from our behavior. We often forget or ignore the truism that what we do has more impact than what we say. The vacuum that is created if we are not our children's moral exemplars will be filled by other influences.

RECLAIMING RESPONSIBILITY

The good news is that we can reclaim responsibility for our children's moral and ethical lives. Moreover, we can do it as Jews. We can do it because Judaism provides both the content and the process for reaching out to our children and for providing alternatives to what secular society has to offer. Furthermore, knowing that we aren't alone, that we are part of a group of like-minded people, strengthens us. Creating expectations and norms that are in consonance with those of our community demonstrates a united front to our children and emphasizes the importance we attach to these values.

"Jews have thousands of years of moral education that has created a people connected to God," explains Helene Z. Tigay, executive director of the Auerbach Central Agency for Jewish Education (Melrose Park, Pennsylvania) and co-founder of three Philadelphia-area programs for teaching moral education. "We have a vision of how individuals and society can live in a holy world, and we have the tools to create sanctity. In today's world, there is a lack of holiness. Universal moral values aren't enough. God is the major part of the fabric of the world. Without God, there is a whole different approach. With God, it isn't just one person's belief, but an ultimate moral plan for the world. It raises everything from the mundane to the holy."

"Judaism has a set of anchored moral values that are exquisite about the kind of life we'd like to lead," says Rabbi Jeffrey Schein, professor and director of family and adult learning at the Cleveland College of Jewish Studies (Cleveland, Ohio) and the national director of education for the Jewish Reconstructionist Federation. He adds, "Judaism's ritual and ethical thrust are supportive of one another, its wisdom has evolved over time, and there is a depth of insight, all of which provide a value system worth communicating."

The goal for Jewish parents who hope to improve their children's moral and ethical life is *menschlichkeit,* the act or condition of being a mensch. What is a "mensch"? It is a person who is more easily defined by experience and example than by the dictionary; we all know one when we have met one. Decent human beings; good, humane people; caring individuals; fully *human* human beings—any of these descriptions will do. The challenge is this: How do we raise a child to be a mensch?

Judaism has long had a viable answer: *middot*—ways of thinking and feeling about ourselves, others, and God that translate into mitzvot, good deeds or specific actions of kindness or helpfulness. A *middah* (the singular of middot) is a virtue, a universal concept that is nonnegotiable. "It is more than a value, a choice we make based on what is important to us, which is culturally normed," Barbara Coloroso explained to me. Middot are Godly acts that elevate us from the mundane.

Middot were first listed in the Book of Exodus (34:6–7), where they are descriptors of God: "compassionate and gracious, slow to anger, abounding in kindness and faithfulness, extending kindness to the thousandth generation, forgiving iniquity, transgression, and sin." A main source of information about middot is *Pirke Avot* ([*Ethics of Our Fathers*] 6:6), which states that Torah is acquired through forty-eight virtues and then proceeds to list them. Yekutiel b. Binyamin Harofe, a thirteenth-century Roman Jewish scribe, included twenty-four virtues in his book *Sefer Maalot Hamiddot* (*The Book of the Choicest Virtues*), the first comprehensive work about the virtues Judaism holds dear. *Orchot Tzaddikim* (*The Ways of the Righteous*) lists both positive and negative traits, with the instruction to study them all and strive to improve oneself. "*Middot* challenge us to raise the level of our interactions with each other, with ourselves, and with God," writes Susan Freeman in *Teaching Jewish Virtues*. "*Middot* might be considered guidelines for how to carry out our deeds. . . . They reflect the intentionality of our efforts and the caliber of our actions."

A *mitzvah*—a much more familiar word to most Jews— is commonly mistranslated as a "good deed"; but it is actually a commandment, one of 613 in the Torah. Deeds or actions that actualize and

concretize the middot, mitzvot are ways of behaving, ritually, spiritually, and personally. "One might see mitzvot as ritual and moral pre-
scriptions—guidelines for what to do, what not to do, and when,"
explains Freeman.

It is possible, however, to perform a mitzvah to the letter of the law
without the virtuousness of the middah infusing it. For example, one
could technically carry out the mitzvah of welcoming guests
(*hakhnasat orchim*) without feeling particularly hospitable. Middot are
difficult, if not impossible, to judge or quantify. How can a person's
feelings and intention be divined? Mitzvot are clear; either an action
has been performed or it has not. Sometimes, we must perform the
action and trust that the feeling will follow.

It is said that "*mitzvah goreret mitzvah*"—that one mitzvah leads to
another mitzvah. That is also true for middot, explains Sharon
Charish, an educator who specializes in teaching about moral virtues.
Likewise, she notes, *mitzvah goreret middah*, and *middah goreret mitzvah*.
Do the deed, and the virtuous feeling will infuse our souls; feel virtuous, and you will likely follow the commandments. Practicing mitzvot
and middot becomes a habit.

Rabbi Richard Hirsch, executive director of the Reconstructionist
Rabbinical Association, explains it this way :

> Middot are attributes, qualities, ways of being. Mitzvot are a
> reflex of the qualities. They are actions, doing that which you
> are obligated, commanded to do. Menschlichkeit is something
> you want kids to internalize so that it becomes their own
> expectation of how they want to be, because eventually it is
> their choice. We hope that living by middot and mitzvot,
> being a mensch will become, in computer language, the
> "default" position. We are training people to have an automatic
> posture that is consistently the best possible response to any
> given situation. So, for example, a person will "default" to a
> position of compassion rather than judgment.

Although Judaism does not have a monopoly on teaching moral and ethical behavior, it does have a unique set of time-tested texts and experiences with which to do so. Judaism also has a language—Hebrew—that is so rich with nuance and meaning that it sometimes actually defies translation. Stories, from the Tanakh, the Talmud, and even from modern Jewish life, as well as prayers and rituals, often establish middot and mitzvot indirectly, through the actions of the character in the tale or the actions we take. The beauty in Judaism is that the rituals, wisdom, and culture are intertwined, one enriching the other.

TEACHING OUR CHILDREN DILIGENTLY

My goal in this book is to help Jewish parents improve their children's moral lives by helping them become menschen. By examining Jewish teachings about menschlichkeit—about middot and mitzvot—we can prepare ourselves to teach them diligently to our children. Of the many middot that have been identified, listed, and discussed throughout Jewish history, I've selected five for inclusion in this book. While an argument could be made for including many other virtues, the ones I discuss seem so fundamental, so significant, that they are a good place for parents to start. For each middah, I discuss several mitzvot that help us exemplify the middah with our deeds.

A note about the interpretations of the middot and mitzvot is necessary here. I explore interpretations of values and behaviors that may stretch these words' meanings so that they are much broader than their strict translations. I have done this to make them more relevant to a wide readership, which I hope will include all Jewish parents. My intention is to help parents relate to them and relate them to parenting. The liberties I have taken are not meant to offend anyone.

Parenting is an art, not a science. There are not many hard-and-fast rules. As parents we often have to go with the flow and react as best we can to a situation, given our own and our children's individual needs and abilities. Sometimes, we choose to guide and teach, other times to allow children to experience the triumph or disappointment of independent efforts. It is almost impossible to be consistent at all times. And sometimes our behaviors may seem inconsistent, even when the intent behind them—to enable and enhance our children's growth and development—is unswerving.

In closing, let me add that I have been an educator for more than three decades and a parent for more than two. The ideas and suggestions I make in the pages that follow have been gathered and developed over all these years and then filtered through the lens of my own experiences. But the touchstone for all my suggestions is the basic teaching of Judaism, that people are created in God's image—*b'tzelem Elokeim*—and commanded to act in ways befitting that creation. Our Torah tells us that God made humankind in the image of God (Genesis 9:6), and it reminds us to walk in God's ways (Deuteronomy 28:9). By practicing middot and mitzvot, we are participating in the ongoing process of creation: We are creating a world in which people treat themselves and each other as God's creatures, as beings of infinite value and worth.

TALKING ABOUT IT

Because becoming a mensch is as much about doing as about studying and thinking, I've included the "Talking about It" sections of this book to get you started. I developed these sections to help adults teach children. Each "Talking about It" contains a traditional Jewish story as well as age-appropriate modern scenarios for the mitzvot presented in that chapter. Each tale, story, and scenario is followed by a list of questions that encourage thinking, discussion, problem solving, and more questions. We parents can and should share our thoughts, experiences, and opinions with our children as they look into their own hearts and examine their own actions. Remember, we teach menschlichkeit best by example.

If we are receptive to and respectful of our children's ideas, even when we disagree with them, the lines of communication will remain open. The goal is to know what our children are honestly thinking and why. Our aim is not to prove to kids that they are wrong and that we have the right answers. All that will accomplish is to convince them not to talk to us in the future. When disagreements occur, we can try to keep thinking and continue talking. In some instances, we may agree to disagree. And if a behavior isn't life threatening, immoral, or illegal, we may want to consider leaving it alone.

I hope the stories in the "Talking about It" sections are catalysts for a change of heart—from which the behavioral changes will naturally follow. I hope they will encourage a long and productive dialogue between children and the adults who love them. I hope we and our children will enjoy our time together, talking about it. ❦

1

Timeless Principles for Teaching Menschlichkeit

So follow the way of the good and keep to the paths of the just
For the upright will inhabit the earth . . .

—Proverbs 2:20–21

I t is a moral imperative: We *shall* teach our children mensch-lichkeit. Judaism does not take a laissez-faire, hands-off approach to parenting. There is no question of our responsibility to introduce our children to a moral and ethical code of behavior; we are com-manded to do so. "Impress them [mitzvot and middot] upon your children" (Deuteronomy 6:7) is the *sine qua non* of responsible Jewish parenthood. Our tradition refuses to let us off the hook. We are obliged to provide our children with what they need to develop into physically, intellectually, morally, spiritually, and psychologically healthy adults. If we do not, we are abrogating our responsibility as parents. Judaism teaches that "The parent is obligated to . . . teach [the child] Torah . . . and to teach [the child] a trade or profession" (Babylonian Talmud, *Kiddushin* 29a). "Some say the parent must also teach the child to swim. . . . What is the reason? His life may depend on it" (Babylonian Talmud, *Kiddushin* 30b). Similarly, our children's existence as fully developed human beings may depend on their learning menschlichkeit.

What a daunting responsibility! How do we know what to say and do? Should we offer advice or keep silent? What are the right words, the correct gestures, the ones that might influence and not irritate? How do we become our children's moral exemplars—wise and ethical people whom our children wish to emulate?

There is an answer. Judaism teaches us how to approach this challenge. Our tradition provides an approach to parenting that is, in itself, menschlich. In essence, we model the outcome through the process. Our children learn menschlichkeit because all they see, hear, and observe of our interactions with them and with others is meschlich. We are their living examples.

From tried-and-true Jewish wisdom, guided by many years of teaching and parenting experience, I have distilled what I consider to be ten timeless principles of teaching—be it menschlichkeit, or anything else. When we follow these guidelines, our process becomes the product.

TIMELESS PRINCIPLE 1: LEARN BY DOING

Judaism teaches what savvy educators have practiced for years: People learn best when they are actively engaged in the learning. When God gave the Jewish people the Torah, their response was "All that the Lord has spoken we will faithfully do" (Exodus 24:7). From this, we understand Judaism's emphasis on action, on participation. And, as a nation of teachers and students, we understand that this is the best way to learn. Practice, the old saying goes, makes perfect. To teach our children about mitzvot and middot, we must engage in them. And although it is important to read about mitzvot and middot, to talk about them, and to think about them, these acts are not enough. We must get out and do them.

Volunteering at a soup kitchen gives privileged teenagers a great deal to think about. Homeless people now have faces, voices, and names. The similarities and differences between the haves and have-nots might never be clearer. And our children experience the answer to Judaism's timeless question, "Am I my brother's keeper?" Helping clean up a park empowers school-age children, while they do something positive for the environment. *Tikkun olam* (repair of the world) becomes more than a slogan; our child knows she can help save the world—at least her little corner of it—because she has actually done so. Even such simple actions as feeding and watering pets regularly teach preschoolers kindness, caring, and responsibility. As Rabbi Abraham Joshua Heschel wrote in *The Theology of Reinhold Niebuhr,* "The act teaches us the meaning of the act."

Doing is commanded in Jewish tradition. "Mitzvah," in fact, means "commandment." Giving *tzedakah* (charity), for example, is not merely a whim or a nice thing to do. We cannot wait until the spirit moves us, for what if we are not so moved? There are always people in need with no one to provide for them. Jews are, in fact, commanded to give tzedakah regardless of whether or not we feel like it. Our rabbis and teachers understood that once an act becomes a habit, it sticks with us. Once our children are accustomed to practicing mitzvot it will be a part of who they are. It will become as natural as breathing. With pleasure and pride in their actions, they will likely look for new ways to participate in helping others.

TIMELESS PRINCIPLE 2:
TARGET YOUR EFFORTS

Modern educators have long emphasized the importance of age, ability, and interest to effect successful education. Judaism knew this long ago. The Bible says, "Train a lad in the way he ought to go; He will not swerve from it even in old age" (Proverbs 22:6). According to Rashi, this means that we must teach each child according to that child's aptitude and capacity for learning and at his or her developmental level. We adapt our lessons for the individual child. No child is too young to begin learning middot and mitzvot, but every child must be approached in a way that he or she can understand. We speak to preschoolers in one fashion, to teens in another. We teach children with disabilities differently from the way we teach children without disabilities. What is crucial is modeling menschlichkeit for all children from their youngest days. They then learn from what they have experienced.

Similarly, no child is too old to learn menschlich behavior. Even if we didn't teach mitzvot when our children were tots, we can still have an effect on a teenager. Of course, we must realize that this may be a difficult task. Teens challenge everything we say and do, as is their wont. Moreover, teens have finely tuned hypocrisy radar; if they suspect that our sudden new interest in mitzvot is merely a means to influence them, we have lost them. We should be living menschlich lives because we want to, because it is the right thing to do, because it enriches our lives, and because it is a moral imperative for Jews. Then, even if our children do not emulate our behavior, we can still feel good about ourselves and our efforts.

Children with disabilities are able and eager to learn about their religious heritage, and we must never neglect or underestimate them. Active, participatory learning about middot and mitzvot cements their connection to their Judaism. Inclusion in a family or community mitzvah project builds fragile self-esteem; it demonstrates to these children and the world that people with disabilities can give as well as receive. This is a menschlich way to teach menschlichkeit.

Parents should know, or discover, how each of their children learns best. Every person has different strengths and weaknesses. One child is an avid reader, while another excels in math. This child loves drama, and that one is a natural athlete. We should identify our children's favorite and most effective learning pathways. Do we show or tell? Do we discuss? Do we read? We must determine how best to approach each of them.

Moreover, we can tap into our children's talents, interests, and hobbies, helping our children perform middot and mitzvot in ways they naturally enjoy. The budding actor should be encouraged to read aloud to younger children or seniors. The athlete can be challenged to raise money for tzedakah by participating in a race for a cure. Such lessons will be pleasurable and, therefore, effective.

TIMELESS PRINCIPLE 3:
TALK THE TALK

To teach our children, we must reach our children. Talking—and listening—to them is one of the best ways to do this. This may sound simple and, perhaps, simplistic—but it is neither.

While most of us have a moral code by which we live, we may never have attempted to teach it to our children or even to have verbalized it. Many of us, for example, give tzedakah. Yet how many of us sit down with our children and explain which causes we support and why? Do we encourage our children to give a portion of their own money to the tzedakah of their choice? Do we have a tzedakah box in which we regularly collect family donations, and do we then discuss together where to give the money?

We need to engage our children as often as possible in discussions about life—ours as well as theirs. We can share our thoughts about moral dilemmas, those sticky situations when two equally good or equally bad alternatives compete with one another. This is where the real moral and ethical learning happens. It's easy to choose between good and bad; it is harder to decide between the lesser of two evils or the greater of two goods. The best learning takes place if parents don't provide the answers but instead offer a forum for discussion. Talking with our kids about things that happen to us, at work or at play, allows them to see us wrestling with ethical and moral challenges. We must not be afraid to let them know that we don't have all the answers; we should allow our children to observe our own learning process. As philosopher Martin Buber wrote, in *Between Man and Man,* "For educating character you do not need a moral genius, but you do need a man who is wholly alive and able to communicate himself directly to his fellow human beings."

One excellent—and very Jewish—way to initiate such discussions is through stories. Judaism has a plethora of biblical, talmudic, and midrashic tales that provide much food for thought. We might read such a story aloud at the dinner table on Shabbat and involve the whole family in the discussion, or we may introduce a tale before bed for an intimate and private time with an individual child.

Current events are another excellent source of discussion topics. Reading newspapers and news magazines or watching the evening news with our children (before or after but not *during* dinner!) can provide the fodder for interesting, and sometimes heated, discussion. What are our children's opinions about a specific story? What does Judaism teach us that seems to be relevant? The deeds of modern "mitzvah heroes"—as author Danny Siegel, in *Heroes and Miracle Workers,* calls them—can be another wonderful focus of discussion. Mitzvah heroes are ordinary people who do remarkable things to better the world. Learning about these people can inspire us to do mitzvot, too.

These conversations can help us see into our children's minds and hearts without our having to ask awkward personal questions about their friends or themselves. The most important part of talking with children, however, is not talking; it is listening. If we listen, we never have to worry about saying the wrong thing! And when we listen to our children with open minds and hearts, we will learn a lot more about them than they'd ever tell us if we questioned them directly. This does not mean that we shouldn't offer opinions; we can and should—perhaps especially if our opinion differs from our children's.

Remember that kids love to debate, so we should let them play devil's advocate and try not to become unduly upset by what they say. Youngsters often find that if they talk something through they will not need to try it out. And, sometimes, they say things simply to shock us and to see if they can provoke a reaction.

When talking with our children, we should be acutely aware of the tone of our voice and our body language. We must monitor our talking-to-listening ratio and try to do less of the former and more of the latter. We should keep in mind that lecturing or pontificating rarely wins friends or influences children. Tolerating our children's opinions teaches them tolerance.

TIMELESS PRINCIPLE 4:
WALK THE WALK

Although talking the talk is important, it is not enough. We must model the behavior we hope our children will emulate. One of the most powerful ways to influence our children is to be the living, breathing, best example we can be. We can't expect our children to do as we say but not as we do. The Talmud teaches, "What a child says in the street is his father's words or his mother's" (*Sukkah* 56b). And likewise, what a child does in the street is a reflection of what he has seen his father and mother do.

In an ideal world, middot and mitzvot are already integral to our lives, and what we teach our children is a natural extension of that fact. That we are living a menschlich life daily and that our menschlich behavior is the essence of who we are make the greatest possible impression on our children. Living the mitzvot provides spontaneous and genuine opportunities to show and tell, to find teachable moments, and to explain our actions and reasoning to our children. Our consistency elevates single actions into family traditions. And these, in turn, become the foundation on which our children will build their own future observance of mitzvot.

If, on the other hand, there is a discrepancy between what we say and what we do, no amount of talking will get our message across. Most children are keenly sensitive to insincerity; if we don't walk the walk, they will discover it and assume that the talk doesn't really matter.

Although it often seems that our children don't pay attention to us, they are really watching us closely and listening to what we say. We may be self-consciously aware of modeling certain types of behavior—volunteering with our children at a recycling center, for example—yet completely unaware of other behaviors that telegraph powerful messages. For instance, if we use a cell phone while driving, our children will get the message that this is an acceptable practice. However, this act demonstrates disregard for human life—ours, our passengers', and the lives of the people in nearby cars. Obviously, this attitude is not what we intend to model for our children, yet many of us engage in this behavior.

Even if our children choose not to emulate our virtuous behavior, walking the walk is still important for our own sense of what is right. And even as our behavior bolsters our self-respect, it will earn our children's respect as well. And remember, the effects of our modeling are sometimes not seen until our children become adults themselves.

TIMELESS PRINCIPLE 5:
FIND A VILLAGE

The expression "It takes a village to raise a child" may have been drawn from African tradition, but it is certainly true of Jewish communities as well. Judaism recognizes the importance of the village to provide support and enthusiasm. For example, to read Torah or recite certain prayers, we need a minyan, which is a group of at least ten people. Providing a sense of community can be a positive force in our children's lives.

Parents should seek an environment filled with people living middot and mitzvot, a moral community. When children see everyone around them acting in accordance with a certain moral code, it lends credence and importance to that behavior. In *Pirke Avot* ([*Ethics of Our Fathers*] 6:9), Rabbi Jose ben Kisma writes, "Though you give me all the silver, gold, precious stones and pearls in the world, I would not live anywhere except in a community where there is Torah." Neither should we.

So who lives in our village? Our immediate and our extended families are in our village. So are our neighbors, friends, fellow synagogue members, business associates, classmates, and teammates. The people with whom we choose to live, work, and play become role models for our children—for good or for ill. It matters that our children hear them talk the talk and see them walk the walk. While we may be scrupulous about our own behavior, our children would be justified in wondering why we associate with people who gossip nonstop or make disparaging remarks about people of different races, religions, sexual orientations or ethnic groups. On the other hand, they also notice when, for example, the parent-coach of their soccer team requests that another parent who is cursing at a referee leave the field. Our children will clearly see that certain behavior is not tolerated in the company with which we want to associate.

Our village may or may not be solely within the Jewish community. Nowadays, few of us live in exclusively Jewish neighborhoods or belong to exclusively Jewish groups. Our children are members of multiple communities, including school groups, scouts, and sports teams and participate in art, dance, and music classes as well. What matters is that our children are surrounded by people who act in ways that support moral behavior.

TIMELESS PRINCIPLE 6:
RESPECT OTHER VILLAGES

Jews have not cornered the market on virtue. Other faith communities teach moral and ethical behavior, and our tradition teaches that "the righteous of the nations of the world have a portion in the world-to-come" (*Tosefta Sanhedrin* 13:2). Being a mensch means respecting all people; and modeling respectful behavior in our daily interactions with others teaches this lesson more clearly than anything we might say. Our children learn to respect other peoples and nations when they see that we do. This is one of the best ways to bring *shalom* (peace) into the world.

It is important to be vigilant about our behavior in this regard, since we are sometimes unaware of actions that display disrespect for other people, faiths, and communities. Some Jewish people, for example, may describe something as having been done in a *goyishe* way. The implication is that it is not only different from but also somehow not equal to the Jewish way of doing it. This phrase, perhaps a thoughtless habit, is disrespectful and belittling. The insult may cut especially deep if heard by a Jew who has converted to Judaism or by members of an interfaith family.

Children also come to respect other communities when they have a chance to learn about them. It is difficult to honor what we don't know or understand. Ignorance can breed misunderstanding, distrust, and fear. When we learn the origins and reasons underlying different customs and traditions, we are more likely to honor them.

Do we have friends of other faiths and ethnic backgrounds? Do we encourage our children's friendships with children of different colors, beliefs, and traditions? Do we visit each other's homes, sharing holidays and traditions? Many schools, camps, and youth groups—religiously affiliated and secular—sponsor programs that promote multicultural learning. Participation in such activities helps broaden our children's horizons, making other people, and their beliefs and customs, familiar and comfortable to them. Our actions in this regard send a strong message to our children. Bridges are built through understanding.

TIMELESS PRINCIPLE 7:
NAME THAT VIRTUE

"Language, the key to a nation's heart," wrote the famous Jewish poet Hiam Nachman Bialak in 1923. Judaism's language, Hebrew, names and describes moral virtues in ways that are so rich with meaning that the English translations barely suffice. Parents can learn to use these words so that they become part of the household vocabulary, a kind of shorthand for valued behavior. It may be eye-opening and empowering for Jewish children to learn that their religion holds definite moral positions and even has a special language of moral and ethical behavior. (For a list of some of these words, see Appendix A.)

When we accompany an action with the explanation—"It's a mitzvah"—we attribute something special to the act. When we say that we give *kavod* (honor) to someone or hope that there will be *shalom bayit* (peace in the household), our children will take notice. They may begin to think about their daily actions as connected to and expressive of their Judaism. This, in and of itself, is a huge step for many children. One highly moral and sensitive teen, when told that her light-hearted gossip constituted *lashon ha-ra* (bad language), thought about it and asked, "Does that mean I'm not a mensch?" Although she was reassured that she was, indeed, a mensch, she also learned that gossip—even the light-hearted variety—is potentially hurtful to others as well as unbecoming to herself.

Parents may feel awkward or embarrassed if they do not know Hebrew or all of Judaism's teachings and traditions. Some may even dismiss the notion that religion can help them be better parents. But Judaism has much to offer adults who are struggling to teach the children they love moral and ethical behavior. When we study with our children, learning both Hebrew and Judaism's ideas about menschlich behavior, we make an extremely powerful statement about what is truly important to us, and it helps emphasize the power of learning— a key Jewish value. When we use the language of our people in our daily interactions, we make a statement about identity and belonging.

TIMELESS PRINCIPLE 8: HAVE HIGH EXPECTATIONS

Parents should expect that their children will try to live moral lives. Such confidence is often a self-fulfilling prophecy; children are likely to live up (or down) to the expectations that the important adults in their lives have for them. Thus we should let them know that we believe in them. After all, as Maimonides wrote in the *Mishneh Torah,* "Every human being is capable of becoming righteous like Moses."

This is a high standard to aim for. We demonstrate an incredible amount of respect for our children when we let them know, through our words and actions, that we regard them so highly. Direct praise for their good decisions is one way to accomplish this. "I'm proud of you; I guess you must be proud of the menschlich way you handled that difficult situation," is a warm, wonderful, and Jewish way to express our pleasure. All too often, we take the good things for granted and comment only on what needs to be fixed or changed. Our praise comes through loudly and clearly to our children and makes a lifelong impression on them.

Our actions can speak even more eloquently than our words. Actions demonstrate to our children that they are fulfilling our high expectations. For example, by giving children who have displayed trustworthy behavior increasingly greater amounts of freedom and responsibility—be it access to the house keys and burglar alarm code for preteens or the car key and a credit card for high schoolers—we graphically and concretely display our trust. And the more we trust, the more trustworthy most children will become. They will like the feeling, and so will we.

TIMELESS PRINCIPLE 9:
EXPECT AND ACCEPT MISTAKES

No one, not we and not our children, is perfect. In *Shirat Yisrael,* Ibn Ezra pointed out, "Perfection belongs only to God." It is human to make mistakes; the challenge is to learn from them. We parents must allow our children to make their own decisions and, therefore, their own mistakes. We must help them understand that mistakes are not only natural but necessary. And we must create an atmosphere in which our children can learn from their mistakes. One very important way to do this is to admit to our own mistakes and demonstrate how they can be a force for our own growth. And when our slip-ups involve our children, we must own up to them and apologize for them, without making excuses.

Parents naturally wish to protect their children from difficulties and problems. Yet in doing so, we sometimes prevent them from learning. We keep them from making choices that we know, with the wisdom of experience, are wrong. But if the consequences of such a mistake will not harm themselves or others, we need to see the situation as an opportunity for learning. And we should allow our children to make their own decisions—and their own mistakes. A child's poor decision may cost time, money, aggravation, a grade, a job, or even a friendship. For some of us parents, this is too high a price, and so we are easily tempted to intervene on our child's behalf. But intervention when our children's actions are not life-threatening or illegal demonstrates a lack of trust and respect for them and for their ability either to work things out or to survive the consequences.

By expecting and accepting mistakes, I mean that we should not catastrophize them. Instead, we need to keep things in the proper perspective and avoid getting upset by small blunders. We should also try to maintain a sense of humor, realizing that some types of mistakes make for funny stories to be laughed at, learned from, and then let go.

One way to help our children learn from their mistakes is to ask questions that open up a dialogue; for example:

• What do you think you should do now? Why? What might be the results?
• What would you do differently next time? Why? What do you think would happen?

These questions don't condemn or belittle, and they don't give children the right (read "our") answers. Rather they help children learn from the process and provide tools for the future.

If children believe that we will accept only perfection, not only will they fail but we will have failed them. We will not be allowing them to be human. One wise parent I know says she wishes people "a good struggle." Parents need to be able to allow their children both a good struggle and the opportunity to learn from it.

TIMELESS PRINCIPLE 10:
TRUST YOURSELF

Fortunately, most parents have good instincts about child rearing, and—despite our general inexperience—most of us do a good job. The important thing is accepting our limitations and ourselves. We cannot and should not constantly second-guess our decisions or feel guilty about what we imagine we could have or should have done differently; most of us do the best we can with the resources we have.

Judaism teaches, "For there is not one good man on earth who does what is best and doesn't err" (Ecclesiastes 7:20). We parents are human; we make mistakes. But we must also trust our efforts.

Parenting is a work in process, constantly evolving and changing, as we change, as our children change, and as the world changes. Judaism provides us a way to think about parenting, a map for the road. Although we each have our own style, as long as we are well meaning, good intentioned, and trying hard, we won't go too far wrong.

Our job as parents is twofold: Maintain the special nature of the relationship that we have with our children and offer them unconditional love. Both are critical to our children's development and to learning and living menschlichkeit.

LIVING WITH PRINCIPLES

When we follow the ten timeless principles and teach our children menschlichkeit, in the menschlich manner that is inherent to Judaism, we are deserving of the blessing that Rabbi Isaac bestowed on Rabbi Nachman. Rabbi Nachman had asked his colleague to bless him. Rabbi Isaac replied, "With what shall I bless you? Shall I wish you Torah learning? You already have learning. Wealth? You already have wealth. Children? You already have children. This, therefore is my blessing: May it be God's will that your children will be like you" (Babylonian Talmud, *Ta'anit* 5b–6a).

2

The Truth, the Whole Truth, and Nothing But

The seal of God is truth.
Babylonian Talmud, *Shabbat* 55a

*E*met (truthfulness) and *emunah* (trustworthiness—not faith in God, as it is usually translated) are among the most fundamental components of menschlichkeit. Judaism teaches, "The seal of the Holy One is truth" (Hanina b. Hama, *Shabbat* 55a). One way to emulate God, in whose image we are created, is to be truthful with ourselves and others. From Psalms (101:7) we learn, "He who deals deceitfully shall not live in my house; he who speaks untruth shall not stand before my eyes." It is impossible to imagine a mensch who lies, a mensch who can't be trusted.

Being truthful with ourselves cleanses and elevates our spirits. Acknowledging our own strengths and weaknesses helps us become the kind of person we aspire to be. We can choose to make changes or to stay the same. Truthfulness with others is the basic building block of relationships, and menschlichkeit is very much about relationships. Truthful words and deeds earn us the trust of our fellow human beings. Our reputation for honesty is priceless; our good name—the assumption that we are truthful and trustworthy—is earned through experience. Once damaged, it is difficult to rebuild.

The importance of emet and emunah should be one of our earliest and most enduring messages to our children. Unfortunately, some of us do not model these values in our own behavior, whether personal or professional. We falsify résumés, pad expense accounts, or take home supplies from the office. Yet Judaism teaches, "A righteous man hates lies" (Proverbs 13:5). We seem to be struggling with the conflict between our Jewish values and our modern lives.

A 2000 study of teen behavior, conducted by the Joseph and Edna Josephson Institute of Ethics (Marina Del Rey, Florida), showed that our children may not understand the importance of honesty. They found that 7 in 10 students admitted cheating on a test at least once, and nearly half admitted to having done so more than once. Furthermore, 92 percent of the 8,600 teens surveyed admitted lying to their parents; 78 percent had lied to a teacher, and more than 25 percent said they would lie to get a job. The study, said Michael Josephson, founder and president of the institute, "reveals a hole in the moral ozone." ("Teens Get Failing Grade in Ethics," by Gisele Durham, *Philadelphia Inquirer,* October 17, 2000.)

The good news is that we can teach children of any age the value of emet and emunah. We can help them become truthful, trustworthy, and trusted people. By teaching our children these basic moral virtues, we give them an essential key to their living menschlich lives.

LEARNING TO TRUST

How do children learn to trust? How do they learn to tell the truth? To be trustworthy, we must first trust others. Children learn to trust from the time they are infants when they have caregivers they can depend on. They learn that when they cry from hunger, someone feeds them; when they scream because they are soiled, someone changes their diapers; and when they howl because they are cold, hot, tired, or in pain, someone attends to their needs. They learn to trust, even before they can speak, because each and every time they need to be taken care of, someone does so. They learn to trust in their primary caregivers and, by extension, the world.

As they grow older, our children continue to trust us when they experience our truthfulness. Even a toddler who is old enough to understand a promise to get ice cream is old enough to understand and feel betrayed when that promise is broken. A commitment to take our children to a ball game or shopping should not be lightly discarded in favor of a chance to play a round of golf or to meet a friend for lunch. Judaism teaches the importance of keeping promises to our children. As Rabbi Zera said, "One should not say to a child, 'I will give you something,' and then not give it to him. He thus teaches the child to lie" (*Sukkot* 46b).

Our failure to honor such promises inadvertently teaches our children two troublesome lessons. First, we demonstrate that telling the truth and keeping promises are secondary to convenience or to a better offer. If it is inconvenient to keep a promise, it's okay to break it. We might make righteous excuses or provide reasonable explanations. But to the child, the message is the same: Keep your promise only if it is expedient to do so. Clearly, that is not a lesson we wish to teach.

Second, we indicate to our children that they are less important than our friends, business associates, or whoever took precedence over them. While a single broken promise may be easily explained and readily forgiven, a pattern of broken promises may leave children feeling hurt, resentful, and devalued. Although this is not our intention, children often react in this manner. And since people often treat others in the way in which they have been treated, children who feel devalued may devalue others, in turn. Moreover, these children may later find it difficult to build adult relationships based on truth and trust.

MOVING OUT INTO THE WORLD

As our children get older, their world expands. As they grow, we hope they learn more about truthfulness and trustworthiness as they observe us modeling these virtues in our daily interactions with family, friends, colleagues, and strangers. Our children are always watching us and listening to what we say. If we teach our children that they should not steal, then we should model that ideal in our own behavior. And while we do not want our children to commit armed robbery at the neighborhood convenience store, we also do not want them to steal on a more personal level.

When our son sees us correct a waiter who has given us too much change, we teach him a lasting lesson about honesty. When we instruct our twelve-year-old to say that she is only eleven so she can get into a movie theater for free, we teach her a lasting, but different, lesson about truthfulness. What do children think when they overhear us discussing how we have hooked into the cable system and are getting our service for free? And what do teenagers learn about honesty when we encourage them to take a job that pays cash and then tell them they do not have to pay their taxes?

Each of these experiences teaches children a lesson about the value we ascribe to truthfulness. If they hear us scoff at others who tell the truth in these types of circumstances or hear us brag about how we beat the system, they learn that honesty is sometimes not important. When we play fast and loose with the truth, can we expect better from our kids?

A story in the Talmud provides a model for this lesson. Rabbi Simeon ben Shetah bought a donkey. When he examined it, he found a precious stone tied to its neck. He returned the stone to the owner, saying that he had bought a donkey, not a jewel (Deuteronomy *Rabbah* 3:3). This is a beautiful example of truthfulness, especially since the other person was unaware of the situation. It is in stark contrast to the "finders keepers, losers weepers" attitude that many of us inadvertently model for our children.

A SELF-FULFILLING PROPHESY

Once our children have learned about emet and emunah through their trust in us, they are ready to be truthful and trustworthy themselves. Young children, of course, may not have a clear understanding of the difference between truths and lies. Toddlers tend to be egocentric and believe that things will be as they think, wish, or want them to be. As they get older, they develop the intellectual capacity to discern truth from fantasy and the emotional capacity to tell the truth more reliably.

Exodus (23:7) tells us, "Keep far from a false charge." But how can we teach this to our children? First, we demonstrate to them that we assume, until shown differently, that they are telling the truth. When we assume the best, children usually live up to our high expectations. Acting on the belief in this kind of positive self-fulfilling prophecy can take parents a long way. It can also teach our children a valuable lesson about human nature.

Second, we can avoid putting our children in situations in which a lie seems like the best alternative. Jewish tradition tells us, "Teach your tongue to say, 'I don't know,' lest you be caught in a lie" (*Berachot* 4a). Children often lie when they are afraid of the consequences an unpleasant truth might bring, be it our disappointment, their embarrassment and humiliation, or some other painful outcome. They think that it's easier, smarter, or more expedient to avoid the truth. Lies, however, beget more lies, and children may find themselves engulfed in a rising tide of untruths.

Our children should know that they can tell us the truth when the unexpected happens—for example, when a friend's party turns out not to have adult chaperones. They should know that they can and should call us for a ride home, no matter the hour, if their driver starts drinking. They need to know they can trust us to react in a supportive and loving way, and we need to know we can trust them to be truthful.

Our loving support, however, must not excuse our children from taking responsibility for their actions. Our kids should know that telling the truth about a negative behavior sometimes requires that they take some compensatory action. Even a young child who hurts a friend can apologize and find a way to make amends. An older child who admits to breaking something can be expected to fix it, pay to fix it, or replace it. If a teenager's transgressions involve more severe infractions, we need to be loving and supportive but not rescue them from responsibility—even if law-enforcement officials have been called in. Parents who hire an attorney, seeking to excuse their children's unlawful behavior and save them from facing the consequences of their actions, are sending a message about truthfulness and honesty. It is not, however, a message that will help their kids grow into "mensch-hood."

One couple found the courage to enforce this lesson when they were called to the police station on a Saturday night because their underage teenage son was picked up with a group of friends who were drinking. One of the boys had gotten so sick that he had begun to vomit and choke. Most of the group fled when they realized the police were coming; only this couple's son and one other boy stayed to help their friend. The parents let their son know that they were angry and upset about the drinking. But they also told him that they were proud of his courage and honesty in staying by his friend. The consequences? The boy had to attend a teen alcohol-abuse program, do community service, and pay a fine from his own hard-earned cash.

WHAT HAPPENS WHEN TRUST IS DESTROYED?

We all know the story of the boy who cried wolf. Jewish tradition teaches, "A liar's punishment is that even when he tells the truth, he is not believed" (Babylonian Talmud, *Sanhedrin* 89b). It can be difficult, and sometimes impossible, to rebuild trust after it has been broken. We must say what we mean and mean what we say, and we must do what we say we are going to do. A breach of trust can be healed only through many honest interactions. It may be a long and difficult road.

This is an important lesson for children as they grow older and more able to be truthful and deal honestly with others. Parents may be quick to overlook their children's broken promises or minor untruths; perhaps we ought not to be so ready to do so. It is unlikely that a friend or future business colleague will be equally as understanding. We are not doing our kids any favor when we teach them that a glib "sorry" corrects all indiscretions. Why should we think that our children will be any more truthful the next time? Children should learn that they must be as good as their word; it is the only way that their word will be valued. An apology is a good starting place; but it may not be the ending place.

Children need to have a chance to work out a way to earn back our trust—and this chance is something that loving parents always give their children. But it is important for kids to figure out how to do this on their own; it is not our responsibility to tell them. They have a problem, and they need to discover a suitable solution. On the other hand, we need to be available to listen to their ideas as they think about how they are going to remedy the situation. Learning about problem solving will stand children in good stead in the future.

THE LITTLE WHITE LIE

Although "the whole truth" is standard in a court of law, it may not always be the best standard for human interactions. Who among us has never told a little white lie? Are these types of lies always wrong? This is often a difficult dilemma for parents, so we are fortunate that our tradition gives us guidance.

Judaism teaches that a lie is permissible in order to make or keep the peace or to preserve human dignity. In the Talmud we read, "Great is peace, seeing that for its sake even God modified the truth" (Babylonian Talmud, *Yevamot* 65b). When Sarah overheard God's messenger telling Abraham that she would have a child, "Sarah laughed to herself, saying, 'Now that I am withered, am I to have enjoyment—with my husband so old?'" Then the Lord said to Abraham, "Why did Sarah laugh, saying, 'Shall I in truth bear a child, old as I am?'" (Genesis 18:12–13). God maintained the peace between husband and wife and saved Abraham's pride in the process.

Another example of a permissible lie is described in an argument that was recorded between the schools of Hillel and Shammai. The Talmud recounts many disputes between these two scholars and, later, between their followers. This argument concerned what one should say about a bride just as she is about to walk down the aisle. The school of Shammai said that the bride should be described just as she is. The school of Hillel, on the other hand, maintained that all brides should be described as beautiful and graceful (*Ketubbah* 17a). At that point, Hillel said, there is nothing to be done if something is amiss. A truthful, but disparaging, comment would serve no purpose except to cause pain.

What is the lesson here? It is that truth must be considered in light of the circumstances and that perhaps some truths are relative, to be found only in the eye of the beholder. In the case of bride, we know that she is always beautiful and graceful to those who love her, no matter what a stranger may think. The school of Hillel may have taken these ideas into account, and its position is accepted as Jewish law. In fact, Jewish law almost always agrees with Hillel's position because Hillel and his followers "were gentle and modest" (*Eruvin* 13b); in other words, for moral considerations.

What should we do when we confront such a dilemma? We should ask ourselves the purpose of the lie: Are we helping another person? What can the person do with the information we provide? Can the person learn and benefit from the truth, told in sympathetic terms, even if it is painful? Or is there nothing that can be accomplished or changed, in which case the truth can only cause anguish?

We should discuss these types of questions with our children. Problem solving together, sharing the story of Abraham and Sarah or discussing the debate about the bride, prepare us and our children to make the best possible decision in similar situations. We could also tell our children about a time when we told a white lie and why. Did we keep the peace? Help a friend? Help ourselves? Protect someone's dignity? And we should ask our children what they would have done in a similar circumstance.

HONEST THOUGHTS AND FEELINGS

Truthfulness demands consistency between what we say and what we believe. The Talmud says, "People should not say one thing with their mouths and something else with their hearts" (*Bava Metzi'a* 49a). Jeremiah (9:7) talks about one who "speaks to his fellow in friendship, but lays an ambush for him in his heart." This aspect of truthfulness may be difficult to explain to children. Kids have trouble understanding why their negative thoughts matter if their actions are correct. Such deception, however, can have a destructive effect on the owner of those thoughts, even when not acted on. This concept may make children feel uncomfortable and guilty as they recognize their hidden dishonesty. We need to explain to our children that thoughts can lead to words and deeds, and it may only be a matter of time before something hurtful occurs as a result of negative thinking. We can discuss intentionality with older children, asking them to reflect on whether their thoughts and feelings support their deeds, and vice versa.

Many of us are reluctant to express anger or annoyance, fearing that these types of negative emotions are somehow unacceptable. Instead, we hide our true feelings and say nothing or lie, smiling and saying that everything is fine. But the negative feelings don't go away; they may even intensify as our resentment builds at feeling forced to deny our true feelings. If we can learn to express our true feelings, calmly, politely, and promptly, we can usually move on with our relationships intact and feel good about being honest.

To teach this to our children, we must model this kind of honesty with them and encourage them to be honest with others. An "I" message expresses how one feels without blame or recriminations and suggests an alternative and acceptable behavior. A child whose friend is always late showing up to walk to school together can be taught to say, "I get upset at being late for school because I don't want to miss work and get a detention. Please let me know if you can't meet me on time, and I'll go on without you." We hope that this type of honesty will help the friend change her behavior. But if not, our child has learned to express her feelings honestly and calmly and can now decide what to do next.

THE MOST DIFFICULT TRUTH

One of the most difficult ways of being truthful is to be honest about ourselves. We are often our own harshest critics or our most shameless apologists. For example, we may underestimate our abilities, selling ourselves short because we are afraid to look foolish or fail. Or we may be too cocky or too proud to ask for help when we need it, refusing to benefit from advice that could help us. And many of us are not honest about our emotions. Some of us need to recognize and deal with our anger, fear, and jealously rather than allow them to control our actions. And others of us do not let ourselves truly rejoice in the good times and savor the positive things that happen to us.

Many of us are in denial about some aspect about ourselves, whether it is our weight, the amount of alcohol we drink, or the amount of time we spend working. One good way to learn to be honest with ourselves is to share our doubts, faults, and weaknesses with our children. This will not lessen us in their eyes; instead it humanizes us and makes our kids realize that everyone struggles with this type of truthfulness. When we take responsibility for our own missteps, our children learn that is acceptable to make mistakes. Furthermore, when they see us admit our transgressions, learn from them, and avoid them in the future, they will learn to do the same. Menschlichkeit demands that we respect and love ourselves enough to be honest with ourselves. If we are not truthful to ourselves, it is difficult to be truthful to others.

As we strive to teach our children moral virtues, we must teach them the importance of emet and emunah—truth and trustworthiness. It is part of the foundation on which menschlichkeit exists.

MITZVOT

There are many mitzvot that help us teach our children about emet and emunah. The mitzvot I discuss here are ones that children can understand and can relate to in their own lives. They are steps along the road to menschlichkeit.

Returning Lost Articles: *Hashavat Avedah*

A news article about a person who finds a wallet on the street and painstakingly traces the owner to return the credit cards and cash always impresses us. Why? Perhaps it is because of the egocentric mentality of our secular culture. Jewish tradition, on the other hand, is unequivocal in teaching that returning lost objects is the right—and required—thing to do.

Torah teaches that it is forbidden to ignore lost property; in fact, it is mentioned twice. In Deuteronomy (22:1–3) we read:

> If you see your fellow's ox or sheep gone astray, do not ignore it; you must take it back to your fellow. If your fellow does not live near you or you do not know who he is, you shall bring it home and it shall remain with you until your fellow claims it; then you shall give it back to him. . . . And so too shall you do with anything that your fellow loses and you find: you must not remain indifferent.

And in Exodus (23:4–5) we learn that we must return even an enemy's lost goods. Whether the owner is friend or foe, we are required to protect the misplaced items and return them to him or her. Moreover, we are admonished against ignoring or pretending not to notice the lost items; doing so is considered theft.

Perhaps this mitzvah can be regarded as a sort of moral baseline for honesty and truth. Recognizing that a found object must belong to someone, there really can be no question of keeping it. Instead, the simple acts of protecting and returning it set a standard for honesty in bigger things. This is a natural place to begin teaching emet to even very young children in a clear, practical way that they can understand. Opportunities are all around: Lost and misplaced toys, books, and clothing invariably turn up in someone else's car, yard, or playroom. We can help our kids collect items that aren't theirs at the close of a play date and return them immediately to the rightful owner, identifying the act we are performing as a mitzvah. Young children can also be helped to recognize their sad feelings when they lose something meaningful or valuable, which can help them empathize with others in the same situation.

School-age children and teens enjoy borrowing one another's clothes, books, games, CDs, and movies. Harmless and fun, this can encourage a child's generous, giving nature. But we may need to remind children that, when the borrowed object seems to have become a permanent fixture, returning it to its rightful owner is important.

Lost money can be a temptation to people of any age. Rabbi Jeffrey Schein, of the Cleveland College of Jewish Studies, tells of imitating the process described in the Mishneh to teach the mitzvah of *hashavat avedah* to his own children. If they found money on the street, he would immediately ask if it was *hefker* (ownerless property). Then he and his kids would problem solve together about how to identify the owner. If the owner was not identifiable, they would give the money to tzedakah, deciding together where to donate it. In this way, Rabbi Schein demonstrated to his children that finders do not become owners by default and that they should not expect to profit from someone else's loss.

Keeping a Promise: *Nedarim*

In Judaism, *nedarim* are legally binding vows, much more significant than the promise made by a child. Yet the essence of Judaism's teaching about keeping one's word is the same: It is sacred. The key principle underlying promises is truthfulness. Judaism is so concerned that we be able to be true to our word that we learn, "It is better to make no vows at all than to make them even if one is certain of fulfilling them" (*Chullin* 2a). We must think seriously about the consequences before we make promises to others and to ourselves.

Almost every day, we make promises that we have every intention of honoring. Yet all too often, the idea that seemed so good at first quickly loses its appeal, or we get busy, or a better opportunity comes our way. As parents, we must remember that if we want our children to keep their word, we need to model this mitzvah. We must keep our promises—large and small—especially those we make to our children. In this manner, we can impress on them, even if they are quite young, the importance of doing what we say we are going to do.

A good exercise is to share our decision-making process with our children. Try thinking aloud about exactly what keeping a certain promise might demand. For example, we can ask, How much time will it take? When must we do it? Can we physically, mentally, and/or emotionally manage it? Can we afford it? How do we feel about doing it? We show our kids that we take promises seriously when they see that we make a plan for how to keep them.

It is important that we hold our children responsible for the promises they make. This requires our physical and emotional presence. If our child is thinking about breaking his word to a friend or to us, we should initiate a discussion that reflects on his feelings, our feelings, and the imagined feelings of his friend when the promise is not kept. "How would you feel if . . . ?" "How do you imagine I feel when . . . ?" and "How do you think your friend will feel about . . . ?" are questions that encourage children to identify their feelings and to empathize with others by putting themselves in another's place. We should also help our child find a way to keep his promise. Ask, "Why can't you keep it?" "What can you do about it?" "How can we help?"

If we ask our children to put their promises in writing, we show them how serious their promises are. These pieces of paper then act as IOUs to remind them of what they've said. Another way to show the gravity of making promises is to shake hands to seal the deal, just as adults do the world over. Young children will likely be impressed by the grown-up nature of a handshake, and teens will like the attitude of trust that it conveys.

NOT STEALING: *LO TIGNOV*

Most of us do not give a second thought to the commandment to not steal. We have never been tempted to rob a bank, and we find it easy to make a moral statement about this kind of blatant disregard for the law and truthfulness to our kids. Stealing, however, may be more subtle and insidious than it appears.

In Leviticus 19:11 we read, "You shall not steal; you shall not deal deceitfully or falsely with one another." The Rabbis teach that this means we should not do anything that might even have the appearance of stealing, whether taking something as a practical joke or even reclaiming our own stolen property, so that we don't seem to be a thief or become accustomed to stealing. We are also told that this means we should not "steal the good opinion of others" (*Mekhilta de-Rabbi Yishmael, Mishpatim*). In other words, we need to earn someone's good opinion of us, instead of trying to acquire it through deception, flattery, or lies.

A common form of modern-day stealing is when we or our children use technology to acquire things that aren't rightly ours. For example, many of us download music off the Internet instead of buying the tapes or CDs; this is stealing from the artists, who make their living from the sale of their music. Some students turn in research papers they've found on the Internet instead of writing their own. This act—as well as cheating on tests, copying homework, and plagiarizing from hardcopy sources—constitutes stealing someone's thoughts, ideas, or intellectual property.

The Rabbis of talmudic times could not foresee computers and the Internet and the ease with which they allow us to access other people's information, but they provided clear guidance on the subject of online, or any other type of, piracy. "It is worse to steal from the many than to steal from an individual, for one who steals from an individual can appease him by returning the theft; one who steals from the many cannot (since he doesn't know all the people from whom he stole)" (*Tosefta, Bava Kamma* 10:14). On the other hand, "Whoever reports a saying in the name of its originator brings the world toward redemption" (*Pirke Avot* [*Ethics of Our Fathers*] 6:6). It is important for children to understand that using a person's words or thoughts without attribution is stealing. It may actually be one of the most damaging types of thefts because it is impossible to return or repay a person's ideas. Furthermore, when we engage in this type of stealing, we have robbed ourselves of the opportunity to pursue our own creative ideas.

We can begin teaching even young children not to steal by setting the example we wish them to follow. Weekly trips to the supermarket are an opportunity to tell children that we must pay first, even though they may see other people snacking on items before checking out. The price of the item is negligible; the price of the lesson is huge.

Engaging older children in a discussion about cheating or downloading term papers is another important way to share our opinions and solicit theirs. This is a real-life problem that all kids face; ask what they think without asking if they or their friends have done it. Share your feelings with them and open up a dialogue, and you may discover, and perhaps even influence, what your teen thinks.

GIVING THE BENEFIT OF THE DOUBT: DAN L'KHAF ZEKHUT

If we are truthful to and trusting of others, we expect them to treat us the same way. Giving someone the benefit of the doubt, expecting honesty and forthrightness, is a way of looking at the world that can become a self-fulfilling prophecy.

Two great rabbis have discussed the problem of rushing to judgment. Hillel said, "Judge not your fellow until you have been in that person's place" (*Pirke Avot* 2:5). This helps us realize that we can never completely understand another person's thoughts, feelings, and motive; we have no way of knowing another person's truth. The Baal Shem Tov noted, "Since you always find excuses for your own misdeeds, make excuses also for your fellow person" (*Derekh Emunah Umaaseh Rav*, p. 59). This reminds us that all of us can make mistakes.

We model this mitzvah with children when we trust them and assume that they are speaking the truth, trying their best, and doing what they have promised. We should encourage older children and teens to adopt this attitude with their friends and classmates. Some of us seem always to be trying to catch our children, especially our teens, in the act of doing something wrong. This bespeaks a lack of trust both in the innate goodness of our children and in their judgment. One savvy and sensitive teen explained that most kids really want to do the right thing and are acutely aware of their failures. Reiterating their shortcomings does not help them change; it only aggravates a potentially explosive situation. Giving children the benefit of the doubt often produces tangible as well as emotional effects.

This can be a balancing act for parents because we are often caught between wanting to be responsible and wanting to trust our children. For example, we know that our children are good kids who stay out of trouble, don't lie, and have nice friends, but at the same time, we know that we need to check that there really will be chaperones at a party. Parents and their children need to work together to find an acceptable arrangement, and children learn that the greater their honesty, the more often they will be given the benefit of the doubt.

TEACHING TRUTHFULNESS
AND TRUSTWORTHINESS

Truthfulness and the trust that develops from it are the lynchpins of human relationships. Without them, true connections between people cannot exist. Children learn to trust from their earliest interactions with their loving caregivers. In turn, they adopt truth as their own standard of appropriate behavior. Telling the truth to others and expecting truthfulness in return becomes second nature. Even in today's world of manipulation, half-truths, and outright duplicity, an honest person is respected. Helping our children earn the right to that respect is our responsibility and our gift to them as we help them develop menschlich behavior.

Talk About It

The only way in which we are able to build successful relations with other people is in an atmosphere of trust. And when our children make mistakes, we do them a lifelong service when we trust their efforts to be better people next time. This helps them learn to be trust-worthy, to trust others, and to give others the benefit of the doubt. One way to begin a discussion about emunah with our children is to ask them to name the people they trust and to explain why they feel they can trust those people. We can also ask them to think about how they themselves demonstrate that they are trustworthy.

Returning Lost Articles

Returning something that doesn't belong to us is an important first step in being a person who can be trusted. We know how terrible we feel when we lose something and should, therefore, understand how bad another person might feel. To help our children start to focus on their feelings in such a situation, whether they are the finder or the loser, we can ask these types of questions:

- Have you ever lost something that is important to you? How did you feel?
- Have you ever found something? What did you do with it? How did you feel?

Moshele's Gift (a Hasidic Tale)

One night, the rabbi was walking through the town and passed the house of Moshele, the water carrier. He heard singing coming from the house and there seemed to be a celebration going on. The rabbi knew that Moshele was a very poor man and he wondered what Moshele was celebrating. The rabbi knocked on the door and asked, "Moshele, what simcha (happy occasion) are you celebrating?"

Moshele answered, "Rabbi, you know I have always been a poor man. Every night at three I go to the synagogue and deliver water for people to wash their hands at the morning prayers. While I'm there, alone, I pray to God to please give me one thousand rubles so that I can buy food for my children and something for my wife to make her life less difficult. In all these years, God has not heard my prayers.

"Two nights ago, I came into the synagogue and found one thousand rubles lying on the floor! I thanked God for finally answering my prayers. But, when I returned to the synagogue last night, I saw a great crowd gathered in front and I asked someone what had happened. 'A catastrophe,' the man answered. 'The community collected one thousand rubles for Chaneleh and her eleven orphans. Now, the money is missing.'

"I went into the synagogue and tried to pray, but I could not. I felt very angry at God. I thought, 'God, if You wanted to give me a thousand rubles, why did You have to take them away from Chaneleh?'

"That night, I couldn't sleep. Then, I thought, 'All my life I have trusted in God. Now, I need God more than ever. I should pray.' Suddenly, I heard a voice saying, 'Moshele, get up and take the money to Chaneleh! It is hers, not yours.'

"I got out of bed, put on my clothes, and quickly took the thousand rubles to Chaneleh's house. When I handed her the money, her face lit up like a thousand candles. And, I was in heaven."

The rabbi, who had listened carefully to Moshele's story said, "But Moshele, now you are poor again."

Moshele answered, "No, Rabbi. God gave me the strength to return the money and my heart is whole again. So, I am very rich!"

- What do you think about what Moshele did?
- Is he rich or poor?
- What would you have done?

What Would You Do?

Preschool Children

At the playground, Jon finds a truck just like the kind that he has been wanting. Jon plays with it and has a lot of fun. When it is time to go home, he wishes he could take it home with him.

- What can Jon can do?
- What do you think will happen?

• What might be a menschlich thing for Jon to do?
• What would you do?

Elementary-School Children

Abby is on her way home from school. She sees a wallet on the ground, picks it up, and looks inside. There's about fifty dollars in cash and a credit card, as well as pictures, a library card, and membership cards for some organizations.

• What are some things that Abby can do?
• What might happen if she does each of these things?
• How does your Judaism help you decide what to do?
• What do you think you would do?

Adolescents

On the floor in the high-school cafeteria, Jason finds a lunch card. To get such a card, a student pays twenty dollars; to use it, he or she shows the card to the cashier and the amount of the purchase is punched out. Only two dollars have been spent on the card Jason finds, and there is no identification on it.

• What are Jason's options?
• What are the consequences of each option?
• What does Judaism suggest we do?
• How would you handle this?

Keeping Promises

It is impossible to trust someone who doesn't keep promises. Judaism teaches that our actions should be as good as our word.

• Do you always keep your promises?
• When is it difficult for you to keep a promise?
• Is there a time that you think it is all right not to keep a promise?

The Weasel and the Well (a Talmudic Tale)

Once, a young girl was walking and lost her way. She came to a well and climbed down the rope to get something to drink. But, when she tried to climb out, she could not pull herself up, and she began to cry for help. A young man who was passing by heard her cries, and he pulled her out of the well. They liked one another and decided to promise to marry when they came of age. "Who will be our witnesses?" the girl asked. Just then, a weasel ran past the well. "Let this weasel and this well be our witnesses," the boy said. "We will promise not to be false to one another."

They parted and went their separate ways. When the girl grew up, she kept her promise. No matter how many men wanted to marry her, she refused. She wanted to wait for the young man she had promised to marry. After a while, she grew so unhappy that she went mad.

The young man did not remember his promise. He married another woman and had two children. Then, two terrible things happened. His first child was killed by a weasel and his second child fell into a well and died. His wife said, "These were not ordinary deaths. Tell me why our children died this way." Then the man told his wife about his promise so long ago. The wife said, "It is clear that you must honor your promise."

The man divorced his wife and returned to the city where the young woman lived. Although she was mad, he said that he would marry her. When he approached her, she did not recognize him. Then, he called out, "Weasel and well!" She instantly regained her reason. They married and were very happy.

- What does this story teach us about the importance of keeping promises?
- What would you do if you made two promises that conflicted with one another?

What Would You Do?

PRESCHOOL CHILDREN

Janet and Lindsey's class is going to the zoo. Janet and Lindsey promised each other to be partners. On the day of the trip, Emily asked Lindsey to be her partner.

- What can Lindsey do?
- What do you think will happen?
- What might be a menschlich thing for Lindsey to do?
- What would you do?

ELEMENTARY-SCHOOL CHILDREN

Ruth promised to lend Jane her notes from science. There is a test tomorrow but Ruth hasn't finished studying the notes yet.

- What are some things that Ruth can do?
- What might happen if she does each of these things?
- How does your Judaism help you decide what to do?
- What do you think you would do?

ADOLESCENTS

Jack promised to play pool with Bob on Saturday night. Then he learned that Linda likes him and is hoping he'll ask her out for Saturday night.

- What are Jack's options?
- What are the consequences of each option?
- What does Judaism suggest we do?
- How would you handle this?

Not Stealing

We know that it is wrong to walk into a store and steal something.

However, there are many other more subtle ways in which people take things that don't belong to them, such as sneaking into a movie without paying.

• Have you ever had anyone steal something from you?
• Have you ever taken something that didn't belong to you?
• How did each of these situations make you feel?

Buried Treasure (a Tale of King Solomon)

Once, a merchant went on a journey. Just before Shabbat, he found himself outside an unfamiliar town. He did not wish to carry money and violate the Sabbath, so he had to think of something to do. Looking around to see that no one was watching, he buried his money under the stump of a tree. Then he went into town to spend Shabbat. But the man who owned the field saw the merchant bury the money, and as soon as he left, the man dug it up. When the merchant returned to get his money after the Sabbath, it was gone.

The merchant went to King Solomon to complain about the theft. The king said, "Find out who owns the field, and tell him that you buried only part of your money in a secret place. Explain to him that you wish to hide the rest of your money, and ask his advice. Should you bury it in the same secret place or in a different place, or should you leave it with a trustworthy person? He will advise you to bury it in the same place so that he can get it. But he will soon realize that if you go to the stump and find the first money missing, you will not want to leave any more money there. Therefore, he will return the money he stole to the hole under the stump."

The merchant did what King Solomon suggested. And, as Solomon predicted, the man who had stolen the money returned it to the hiding place, expecting that the merchant would soon leave the rest of his money there, and he would increase his profits. But that night, the merchant removed all the money and went on his way. The next day, the thief found only an empty hole.

- Do you think it is acceptable to try to outwit a thief in the way that King Solomon recommended?
- Is there ever an acceptable reason for taking something that doesn't belong to you?

What Would You Do?

PRESCHOOL CHILDREN

Max sees a plate of cookies on a table in the lunchroom at his preschool. He would really like to have a cookie.

- What can Max do?
- What do you think will happen?
- What might be a menschlich thing for Max to do?
- What would you do?

ELEMENTARY-SCHOOL CHILDREN

Rich buys a sandwich, fries, soda, and a brownie from the school cafeteria. He pays with a ten-dollar bill, and the lady at the cash register gives him change. When he gets to his seat, he discovers that she gave him too much money.

- What are some things that Rich can do?
- What might happen if he does each of these things?
- How does your Judaism help you decide what to do?
- What do you think you would do?

ADOLESCENTS

Hilary is working on her college-entrance essays. She finds an online site that has sample essays—some on just the topic she has chosen. She knows she can write a great essay, but she doesn't think she has the time. She could use pieces of several essays and put them together.

- What are Hilary's options?
- What are the consequences of each option?
- What does Judaism suggest we do?
- How would you handle this?

Giving the Benefit of the Doubt

When we give someone the benefit of the doubt, we assume that they are going to be honest with us and that they will do what they say they are going to do. It is a way of looking at the world that helps build trust between people.

- How do you feel when someone trusts you?
- Is it a responsibility that you like?
- How do you feel giving someone else the benefit of the doubt?

The Lion, the Mouse, and the Snare (a Story from the Diaspora)

Once a lion was sleeping in the desert when a mouse stepped on his paw and woke him. With one slap of his giant paw, the lion pinned the mouse by the tail and roared, "Your time has come. Why did you wake me?"

The mouse squeaked, "I know I was foolish, but I didn't do it on purpose. Let your anger give way to kindness. Why should a creature as powerful as you bother to crush a little mouse?"

The mouse's words softened the lion's heart, and he decided to let the mouse go. "You won't regret this," the mouse said. "I will repay you one day." The lion laughed at the mouse's bold boast and went back to sleep.

Some time later, the lion fell into a hunter's trap. The more he tried to escape, the more entangled he became. The mouse heard him roaring and rushed to help him.

"The time has come to repay you," the mouse said. He called all of his brothers and sisters, and together they gnawed on the strands of the net with their sharp teeth. The lion was soon free and he bounded back to his lair unharmed.

∽

- Why did the lion give the mouse the benefit of the doubt?
- When have you given someone the benefit of the doubt?
- How did you feel?
- How did things work out in the end?
- How did you feel then?

What Would You Do?

PRESCHOOL CHILDREN

David and Robert are playing with trading cards. After Robert goes home, David finds that one of his cards is missing.

- What can David do?
- What do you think will happen?
- What might be a menschlich thing for David to do?
- What would you do?

ELEMENTARY-SCHOOL CHILDREN

Susan and Marla each have a collection of bead bracelets. One day, Marla finds her favorite silver bead bracelet is missing. She thought that Susan's silver bracelet was broken but remembers that Susan was wearing a silver bead bracelet when she left for school.

- What are some things that Marla can do?
- What might happen if she does each of these things?
- How does your Judaism help you decide what to do?
- What do you think you would do?

ADOLESCENTS

Judy was inviting about thirty friends to a party. She hesitated to invite Josh, because she knows that he smokes pot, and she doesn't want that at her house. Josh said that he wouldn't bring pot to the party.

- What are Judy's options?
- What are the consequences of each option?

• What does Judaism suggest we do?
• How would you handle this?

Telling the Truth

Sometimes it is very difficult to tell the truth, the whole truth, and nothing but the truth. We are afraid of offending people or that there might be a negative consequence for something we have done. Yet, it is impossible to build trusting relationships when we are not truthful.

• Have you ever been afraid to tell the truth?
• How does that feel?
• How do you feel when you do tell the truth?

The Strongest Thing in the World (a Story from the Second Commonwealth)

Darius, the king of Persia, had three bodyguards—a Persian prince; a Hindu prince; and Zerubbavel, a Jewish prince. One night, the three men decided to hold a contest. "Let us each declare what is the strongest thing in the world. When the king awakes he will choose which of our answers is the best," they agreed.

They each took a piece of paper and wrote down their answers. The Persian wrote, "Wine is the strongest thing in the world because it banishes sorrow and gives birth to joy."

The Hindu wrote, "The word of the king is the strongest thing in the world, for all must bow to his will or die."

Zerubbavel wrote, " The power of woman is the strongest thing is the world, for she can humble even kings. But stronger than all these things is Truth, because the earth requires it, the heavens acknowledge it, and all of creation kneels before it. It is perfect. To it belongs power and glory. Blessed be the God of Truth."

They placed their pieces of paper under the king's pillow and left. When the king awoke, he called all of his advisers to hear the words of his three bodyguards. The first two bodyguards defended their answers, and all of the advisers praised them. But when they heard

Zerubbavel's answer they all cried out, "Mighty is Truth! Nothing can compare to it!"

Then the king turned to Zerubbavel and said, "You have won the contest. What do you wish? Name your prize."

"Only one thing do I desire, your majesty," Zerubbavel answered. "I wish to lead my people out of captivity back to their home, and to rebuild God's Temple in Jerusalem. Allow us to leave and to take with us the holy vessels taken by Nebuchadnezzar."

"Granted," the king said. Zerubbavel led the captives home to Jerusalem, and they rebuilt the Temple. Then Zerubbavel, which means "planted in Babylon," received his Hebrew name, Nehemiah, which means "comforted by God."

- Why is the truth so powerful?
- How do you feel when you tell the truth?

What Would You Do?

Preschool Children
Shoshana saw Avi knock one of Mom's Shabbat candlesticks off the shelf. It broke. Avi put the pieces back and walked away.

- What can Shoshana do?
- What do you think will happen?
- What might be a menschlich thing for Shoshana to do?
- What would you do?

Elementary-School Children
Joshua told his school friends that he is the starting pitcher on the Little League team. The coach isn't going to start him in the championship game, but everyone wants to come and watch him play.

- What are some things that Josh can do?

• What might happen if he does each of these things?
• How does your Judaism help you decide what to do?
• What do you think you would do?

ADOLESCENTS

Sarah's school allows students to use a computer for essay exams. Sarah knows kids in her English class who have found a way to cheat on their midterm exams by writing an essay in advance and saving it to the school computer's hard drive. Then they can access it during the exam.

• What are Sarah's options?
• What are the consequences of each option?
• What does Judaism suggest we do?
• How would you handle this?

Living with Truth and Trustworthiness

Emunah is one of the keys to successful human relationships. If there is no trust, it is difficult to build and maintain a bond with someone. We parents should encourage our children to think about how good it feels when someone trusts them and they trust him or her. We should help our children learn to live truthful lives. If we work on making ourselves trustworthy, we will soon find ourselves building trust in all of our relationships.

3

Respect: The Gift That Keeps On Giving

*Let the honor of your fellow person
be as dear to you as your own.*
—Rabbi Eliezer, *Pirke Avot* (*Ethics of Our Fathers*) 2:15

Comedian Rodney Dangerfield used to bemoan the fact that he didn't "get no respect." Some parents probably feel the same way. Respect or honor—*kavod* in Hebrew—is a concept that seems almost quaint, somehow old-fashioned. Yet, respecting one another is essential to all human relationships. Our conduct is an expression of the recognition that all people are to be honored because we are all created in the image of God. To be a mensch means to honor our fellow human beings as we honor ourselves and God.

Kavod is so crucial to human and humane interaction that God requires it of us. "This is what the Holy One said to Israel: My children, what do I seek from you? I seek no more than that you love one another and honor one another" (*Tanna d'Vei Eliyyahu Rabbah* 26:6). According to the Talmud, kavod is expressed through positive deeds. To honor someone or something we must take action; not only is it a matter of feeling a certain way but we must demonstrate those feelings in tangible behaviors. Judaism teaches us to engage in deeds that are respectful of ourselves and others, with the understanding that sometimes feelings follow, rather than precede, actions.

Our children's respect for others grows from their initial love and respect for us. When we love and respect our kids, they learn to respect themselves. And from those feelings and from watching our interactions with others, they soon learn to respect people outside the family. In addition, children find that when they give kavod, they get kavod in return.

WHO AND WHAT DO WE HONOR?

Pirke Avot (2:15) teaches that the honor of another person should be as dear to us as honor for ourselves. Thus we learn a crucial lesson about kavod: Our own honor is primary. We cannot honor others if we do not honor ourselves, and we cannot honor ourselves if we have never experienced kavod. Self-respect is the spark that grows into the flame of respect for others.

In Judaism, self-respect and respect for others are based on the belief that all people are created *b'tzelem Elokeim* (in the image of God). This suggests that there is something God-like, something holy, something divine in each of us. And even though there are times when we do not reveal our best selves—our Godliness—because we are angry, impatient, or careless, we can still honor the divine core that is in each of us.

It is important to teach our children to honor people who look, sound, and behave differently from them; who have a different lifestyle from theirs; and who belong to other religions and social groups. Although most of us find it easy to talk to our children about honoring others, we may find it more difficult to model this behavior. While we may not tell ethnic jokes, we may be sending inadvertent messages to our children when we look disapprovingly at others who do not meet our ideals, such as the homeless, the poor, or people struggling with addiction. We may imply to our children that certain jobs are somehow less honorable than others. Or we are impatient and intolerant when conducting business with employees instead of owners.

We need to help our children understand that honoring themselves is not the same as being conceited, self-indulgent, or selfish. Instead, they honor and respect themselves by recognizing that their own unique bodies, minds, talents, and personalities were created by God in God's image. Our children should understand that they can honor themselves by being careful about what they eat and drink. We parents can help our kids learn that they show respect for themselves when they refuse to do something that makes them nervous or uncomfortable. And from this, they learn to respect such decisions made by their friends and classmates and thus learn to honor others. It is especially important that our teenagers are aware that it is their right and responsibility to make decisions that show respect for themselves—it may even save their lives.

Judaism also teaches us to respect the earth. We are the recipients of a wondrous world that we did not create. By being responsible caretakers of the earth, we honor God and God's creations. Our children show respect for the physical world when they help recycle our cans and bottles and take an interest in saving endangered species. Through these efforts our children learn that the world doesn't belong to them and that they are simply its caretakers.

HOW DO CHILDREN LEARN KAVOD?

Children learn kavod much the same way they learn anything else: by experiencing it. Our children observe us honoring our spouses, friends, family, colleagues, and other members of the community. And they feel pleasure when we honor them. Kids who have received respect will be more likely to respect others. Some of us wonder why adults should honor children, when we've been told that it's the children's responsibility to honor their elders. We parents should honor our children simply because they exist, because they were created *b'tzelem Elokeim*.

So how do we parents show honor and respect for our children? Honoring our babies means paying loving attention to them and taking their needs seriously. We respond promptly to their cries of distress or exclamations of pleasure. We touch them gently and respectfully as we feed, diaper, and clothe them. We respect our toddlers by allowing them to make some of their own decisions; for example, we let them pick out what to wear, even if the colors of their chosen outfit don't quite match. We respect them by not joking about monsters under the bed or their fear of dogs, while gently helping them face and conquer those fears.

We honor our school-age children by listening carefully and respectfully to their opinions about friends, activities, school, music, hairstyles, clothes, and more. Even when we disagree, listening attentively demonstrates kavod. And it has the added benefit of allowing us to be our kids' sounding board while they formulate their ideas about the world.

We honor our teens by respecting their growing maturity and their strong opinions on difficult subjects such as dating, driving, drugs, alcohol, sex, college, and career. One way of teaching our children to respect and honor our opinions and concerns about these topics is to respect and honor theirs. In this way, we parents can keep the lines of communication open. We must guard against pushing our teens into a position that they do not really believe in; we don't want to force them to say yes (or no) just to prove to us that they can. Instead, by showing our children that we honor them and their maturing judgment and opinions and that we have faith in them, they will, we hope, make decisions that are based on kavod.

ARE THERE LIMITS TO HONOR?

Judaism teaches us to honor all people, even people we do not particularly like, including our "enemies." "If your enemy falls, do not exult," we read in Proverbs (24:17). When the Egyptians who followed the Israelites out of Egypt were drowning in the Red Sea, the angels sang in happiness. God rebuked them saying, "My people are suffering and you rejoice" (*Sanhedrin* 39b). Thus, because we are all God's creatures, we must be honored. We can teach our children not to gloat when someone they dislike loses the election for class president or misses a goal on the soccer field. Modeling good sportsmanship in a contest of any kind is a perfect way of demonstrating kavod to our youngsters.

Many of our children wonder what the limits of kavod are. They ask, "What if a friend wants me to lie for him or help him cheat? Can I still honor him if I refuse?"

Judaism teaches that we are not required or expected to transgress for anyone else—not even for a parent—and that we must honor ourselves first. The *Kitzur Shulkhan Arukh* (143:11) says, "If a child is told by his father not to speak to, or forgive, a certain person with whom the child wishes to be reconciled, he should disregard his father's command." No one can insist that we act counter to our consciences or to mitzvot. We can, however, decline respectfully. The Talmud teaches, "If a child sees a parent breaking a commandment, the child is not to say, 'You have transgressed.' Instead, the child should gently ask, 'Is it not written in the Torah thus?' But aren't both expressions equally insulting? So what he should really say is, 'Father, the Torah says such-and-such' [and let the father draw his own conclusions]" (Babylonian Talmud *Sanhedrin* 81a). We must help our children find a respectful way of redirecting, correcting, or refusing to participate in something they know is wrong.

WHAT GOES AROUND

When we truly respect others, it comes from a place deep inside ourselves that has to do with honoring God and all of God's creations. We do not offer kavod as a ploy to get something (honor and respect) in return. Yet when we treat others with respect, they are more likely to respect us. And the more honorably we behave, the more honorable we become. When both our attitude and our actions model a respectful and honorable worldview, we are teaching our children about kavod.

MITZVOT

To teach our children about kavod, we begin by teaching them to honor themselves. Then we encourage them to honor those who are close to them: family, friends, and teachers. Finally, we help them make the commitment to honor all people, other creatures, and the physical world.

Taking Care of One's Own Body: *Shemirat Haguf*

Our tradition maintains that before we can honor others, we must honor ourselves. The most basic way of respecting ourselves is by *shemirat haguf,* taking care of our bodies. Because we are created in God's image and our bodies are a gift, we have a responsibility to maintain our health and well-being. Maimonides (*Code* 4:1) cautions that "it is man's duty to avoid whatever is injurious to the body and cultivate habits conducive to heath and vigor." Judaism teaches that we are not free to do whatever we want to our bodies. In our modern world, we and our children are confronted by high-risk behaviors and debilitating conditions that affect our physical and mental health. Some, like engaging in smoking, drinking, taking drugs, practicing unsafe sex, and driving recklessly, are obviously counter to respecting ourselves. But this obligation also tells us to treat what is treatable, including conditions such as hypertension, high cholesterol, eating disorders, and depression.

Healthy self-care routines are among the earliest skills we can teach our children. We can explain to our toddlers that proper toileting, bathing, and dental care are all ways of showing kavod for ourselves. Our teens should understand that getting enough sleep, engaging in proper exercise, eating right, and keeping annual doctor's appointments are all part of having self-respect. We parents should help our kids understand that Judaism has something to say about their physical well-being and why.

We can teach our children that we and our bodies are God's creations and that we should we thankful for these gifts. In Psalms (139:14) we find one way to express this: "I praise You, for I am awesomely, wondrously made; Your work is wonderful; I know it very well." In a common morning prayer, Jews thank God for "removing sleep from my eyes and slumber from my eyelids," for "making firm a person's steps," and for "giving strength to the weary." And this prayer specifically blesses God who "has made our bodies with wisdom, combining openings and closing—arteries, glands, and organs—into a finely balanced network." The prayer also acknowledges that "should but one of them, by being blocked or opened, fail to function, it would be impossible to exist."

We can encourage our youngest children to name things about their bodies that they are thankful for, helping them develop a positive self-image. We can teach our school-age children that Judaism prohibits us from doing anything that will hurt or endanger our bodies. And we can help them see that it's a mitzvah to eat right, to be careful when crossing the street, and to wear a helmet when riding a bike. Our older children should understand that they honor themselves when they refuse to drink and drive, to take drugs, and to practice unsafe sex. And, although it may not deter them, teens might be interested to learn that Judaism prohibits tattoos and body piercing. In Leviticus (19:28) it says, "You shall not make gashes in your flesh . . . or incise any marks on yourselves."

Another guiding principle in Judaism is moderation; too much of a good thing can be a bad thing. For example, our teenagers become sick from diets that have developed into anorexia or bulimia. Proverbs (25:16) teaches us, "If you find honey, eat only what you need, lest, surfeiting yourself, you throw it up." Thus when we teach our kids the benefits of a healthy diet and regular exercise, we must be sure to encourage safe practices in moderation.

One of the most effective ways that we parents can teach kavod is to model it. Our kids will not take our words seriously if they see us smoke cigarettes or cigars, overindulge in alcohol, or rely on prescription drugs. On the other hand, if we undergo regular physical examinations and dental cleanings, if we work hard to eat right and maintain a healthy weight, our kids will learn that we respect and honor our own bodies. When we exercise together as a family or when we ask our kids to help create some healthy menus, we start them on the road to kavod.

Our children, especially our teens, are likely to disagree with us on important health issues. They want to do what their friends are doing, and we know well the power of peer pressure. They also feel invincible; although they learn the dangers of cigarettes, alcohol, drugs, and unsafe sex in school, they never think that they will be the ones to get hooked or sick. Talking with our children about these issues is critical. Sometimes we are afraid that we will give our kids ideas that haven't yet occurred to them; however, that is highly unlikely in today's world of easily available mass media. Some of us are uncomfortable talking about these types of concerns, but a tried-and-true rule of communicating with our children is to listen carefully to what they are saying and asking and then simply to answer their questions. Although we may not always be able to change their minds, we can demonstrate our kavod for their opinions, a crucial first step to approaching our children on these sensitive issues.

When dealing with our older children, it is critically important that we clearly express our concerns and set definite boundaries when their behavior is dangerous to themselves or others. We must insist, for example, that they wear seatbelts in the car at all times. We should forbid them to go to unchaperoned parties, and should speak out strongly about drinking, smoking, drugs, or sex.

We parents also need to recognize when we have no power to impose our ideas and opinions. Although we want our children to eat healthy food and avoid too much sugar and fat, we cannot control individual tastes and we cannot regulate every morsel our kids ingest. We also need to recognize that moderation is often the best path; we do not want to restrict our children's diets so much that they do not feel comfortable eating birthday cake at a friend's party. We should remember to save our influence and emotional capital for the important issues, so that when we talk about sex, smoking, drinking, drugs, and seatbelts our kids won't tune us out—there, we give no quarter; their lives are at risk.

When we do not have the skills to safeguard our children's health and well-being, Judaism provides more good advice: "When a person has a pain, that person should visit a physician" (*Bava Kamma* 46b). None of us hesitate to take our young children for regular checkups and shots. We usually manage to get our older children and teens to the family doctor for back-to-school, camp, or sports physicals. However, sometimes we hesitate to seek help for children who are having intellectual or emotional difficulties. We may be reluctant to acknowledge those problems or perhaps we may even feel a bit guilty or embarrassed. We tell ourselves that "it's just a phase," "he'll grow out of it," or "the teacher is exaggerating; she isn't doing anything that bad."

However, we do need to find a way to help our children if they are not learning to manage their thoughts and emotions constructively. Sometimes all our children need is the opportunity to talk to a neutral party such as their rabbi, teacher, or guidance counselor or even an adult friend. But sometimes our children need more intensive and extensive professional help. When we have a kid who is having trouble developing mental and emotional health, we must intervene; our actions may save our child's life.

HONORING YOUR FATHER AND MOTHER: *KIBBUD AV VA-EM*

The first four commandments address our obligations to God. The final five speak to our responsibilities to one another. The fifth commandment, to honor your father and mother (Exodus 20:12), is a bridge between them. This position of importance indicates that honoring our parents is tantamount in Judaism to honoring God. It is one of the few mitzvot in the Torah that is reinforced with a promise: "that you may long endure on the land that the Lord your God is assigning you." Moreover, according to the Mishnah, honoring one's parents is one of the few mitzvot that is rewarded both in this world and in the World to Come (*Pe'ah* 1:1). The commandment applies to adoptive parents, step-parents, or anyone else with parenting responsibility; Jewish tradition teaches that the one who raises a child and teaches that child Torah is to be honored as much as a birth parent (*Sanhedrin* 19b).

The commandment tells us to "honor"—not to "love"—our parents, even though we are commanded to "love our neighbor"

(Leviticus 19:18) and even strangers (Leviticus 19:34). Perhaps this is because an emotion as intense as love for one's parents cannot be produced on command, whereas deeds of honor and respect can, even if one is not feeling particularly loving. The Rabbis taught that the best way to honor our parents is by performing positive acts, or doing things for them that they need, such as providing them with food, drink, and clothing (*Kiddushin* 31b). Leviticus (19:3) also tells us to revere our parents, which the Rabbis interpreted to mean avoiding negative acts or things that cause our parents distress, such as not sitting or standing in their customary place, not siding with their opponents in a dispute, and not contradicting what they say (*Kiddushin* 31b).

In today's world, we parents should think about what we need from our children and what is truly important to us in our relationships with them. In this way, we may be more judicious in our interactions with them and may be better able to sift through the nuisance stuff so that we can focus on life-value issues. We need to remember that conflict with our children—especially as they begin to assert their independence—is natural. The trick is to negotiate this challenging period while still maintaining our underlying kavod for each other.

When we have an inherent respect for our children, we are likely to receive respect from them. When we model honor and respect for our own parents and grandparents, we teach our children to respect us.

From the time children are young, we can identify specific actions that demonstrate respect and disrespect to us. We should teach our children that positive actions—which make life more pleasant—demonstrate respect; and these actions include not only being polite to us but also taking out the trash and shoveling the snow. And while Jewish law does not insist that our children always obey or agree with us, it does require that they disagree respectfully. Children of all ages should learn that sarcasm, screaming, and name calling are disrespectful and unacceptable.

HONORING THE ELDERLY: *KIBBUD ZIKAYNIM*

In America's youth-oriented society, the unfortunate equation seems to be more birthdays equals less respect. Other modern cultures, by contrast, treat their elders with well-deserved kavod. Our Jewish tradition reinforces this virtue, noting that long life is a blessing and a reward for living righteously. Lack of respect to the elderly is considered to be so serious that one of the reasons the Temple was destroyed was that "no respect has been shown to the elders" (Lamentations 5:12). Isaiah (3:5) describes a dishonest generation as one in which "The young shall bully the old."

Judaism teaches that elderly people are to be respected for their wisdom and experience. We are told that a person who learns from the young is like one who eats unripe grapes and drinks wine from a vat, but a person who learns from the old is like one who eats ripe grapes and drinks wine that is aged (*Pirke Avot* 4:26). In the Talmud, we read, "It is always the elders who uphold Israel. When does Israel stand upright? When they have their leaders with them. For one who takes counsel with the old never falters" (Exodus *Rabbah* 38). Furthermore, we are taught that even those whose capacity is diminished must be treated with honor: "Even the old man who has forgotten his learning must be treated tenderly" (*Sanhedrin* 96b).

We can engage our children by helping them discover ways to show respect to older members of our family. Young children can simply enjoy being with their grandparents, great-aunts, and great-uncles, sharing an abundance of attention and love. School-age children can start to have more mature relationships with their grandparents, reading, cooking, and playing together. And teens have not outgrown the need for their grandparents' influence and can enjoy a very grownup relationship with an empathic grandparent.

Today, many grandparents and grandchildren do not live in the same city. But if we arrange periodic visits, we can help our kids bridge the gap. In between those visits, we can encourage our children to stay in touch with their grandparents by sending e-mail, making phone calls, and writing letters. The more contact our kids have with their grandparents, the better chance they have to respect and honor them.

Children who do not have elderly relatives can be given the chance to show kavod for seniors who are not related to them. Even very young children can make drawings or cards to send to older neighbors or members of their synagogue. We can take our school-age children to visit and/or volunteer at senior centers and nursing homes. These kids can read to, play games with, or simply talk to lonely people whose days are brightened by their presence. Teens can be encouraged to show kavod for elderly friends and neighbors by helping them around the house or yard or by running errands for them.

HONORING TEACHERS: *KIBBUD MORIM*

Although the days of bringing an apple for the teacher are long gone, respect for teachers is a virtue that Jews—lovers of learning, the People of the Book—emphasize to their children. Judaism teaches that "An ignoramus can not be a fully pious person" (*Pirke Avot* 2:5). Gifted and caring teachers help us find and use the keys that unlock the mysteries of the universe. They challenge us to think, question, explain, wonder, critique, and create. They don't let us off easily but prod us to be the best that we can be. In *Pirke Avot* (4:15), we read, "The reverence for your teacher should be as great as your reverence for God."

Unfortunately, many teachers today, both in secular and Jewish schools, do not feel respected. They report that, too often, we parents are not cooperative partners in working for our children's education. We may forget to return phone calls or may be too busy to come to meetings and school events. Sometimes we do not model kavod for our children's teachers, either by failing to support their recommendations or by not being respectful of them. Remember that most teachers want to work with us to provide a supportive learning environment for our children.

When we set up conferences that include our children and their teachers, we have an opportunity to model a respectful working relationship. Allowing our children to observe and participate teaches them essential life skills in problem solving. Moreover, our children feel respected when their opinions are sought about vital matters regarding their lives and educations.

The mitzvah of honoring teachers extends to the coaches, referees, guidance counselors, youth leaders, librarians, scout leaders, and camp counselors who interact with our children at school and camp as well as on the playing field. To teach our children to respect these adults, we must model that respect for them, acting as living examples of politeness.

CLEAVING TO FRIENDS: *DIBUK HAVERIM*

"Woe betide him who is alone and falls with no companion to raise him," we read in Ecclesiastes (4:10). Friendships make life, if not worth living, certainly more enjoyable. One of the most valuable lessons we can teach our children is how to be a friend; if they are a friend to others, then they will almost certainly have a friend. As Jewish tradition teaches, "What is in your heart about your fellow man is most likely in his heart about you" (*Sifrei Devarim, Piska* 24). Friendship is a precious commodity, not easily earned but easily lost. We need to teach our children how to keep their friendships open and honest, kind and supportive.

True friends are those with whom we can be honest. We can confide the truth about ourselves in them and trust that they will continue to love us. And we can tell our friends the truth about themselves; however, we need to guard against insulting or injuring them and should always be loving and empathic.

We parents can help our children to appreciate good friends and to evaluate what qualities are desirable in a friend. One way to do this is to have strong friendships ourselves with people who have these desirable attributes. We can also ask our kids what they particularly like and dislike about their friends. If we listen carefully to what they say, we can help them begin to reflect on each friend's behavior and on whether each relationship is beneficial or harmful to them. By talking—and listening—to our kids, we can learn the positive behaviors of their friends, including sharing, helping others, and giving support. We can also learn about the negative aspects of their friends' actions, such as hitting, doing drugs, or teasing. Sometimes our children enjoy the friendship of a child the rabbis would call a *haver ra,* a friend who is good company but leads our kids astray. When we learn that our children have befriended such a child, we have the responsibility to discourage that relationship, if possible.

We can discuss the dilemmas of friendship with our older children. For example, we can help our daughter learn what to say when a friend asks whether she likes a new dress, and she hates it. Together, we can figure out how our daughter can be honest while respecting and honoring her friend. Or we can help our son find a way to refuse to go to an unchaperoned party at which there will probably be alcohol and drugs while still showing respect for his peers. These are challenging problems for our children who are still learning about their own boundaries but who want to maintain their friendships. We might role-play these difficult situations with our children, inventing possible scenarios and exploring different ways of handling them.

HONORING ALL PEOPLE: *KAVOD HABRIYOT*

Judaism teaches that honoring all people is what God wants from us. "People must love their fellow creatures and not hate them. The people of the generation that was dispersed all over the earth [Babel] (Genesis 11:1–9) loved one another, and so God did not destroy them but only scattered them. But the people of Sodom hated one another, so God destroyed them from this world and from the World to Come" (*Avot de-Rabbi Natan* 12, 26b). We honor one another for no other reason than that we are God's creatures, created in God's image. Moreover, when we honor other people, we become more honorable and more worthy of respect.

We should not evaluate people's looks, intelligence, wealth, athletic prowess, or some other arbitrary standard to determine their worth.

Judaism teaches that it is not these attributes, but people's humanity that matters. Furthermore, the measure of a society, and of each of us, is demonstrated by how we treat the weakest and most vulnerable members of that society. In Exodus (22:21) we read, "You shall not ill-treat any widow or orphan." And in Leviticus (19:14), we learn "You shall not insult the deaf, or place a stumbling block [lo titeyn mikhshol] before the blind. You shall fear your God." In other words, we cannot be menschen if we are mistreating, or even ignoring, those among us with physical, mental, or emotional disabilities.

We parents should teach our children that despite the advances that people with disabilities have made in American society, misunderstanding, prejudice, and even fear still remain. Judaism teaches us that we all have a responsibility to remove stumbling blocks from our community. We can help our children make a real difference by encouraging them to try to evaluate places and events from the viewpoint of people with disabilities. For example, we can teach our kids that we show honor and respect when we make our sanctuaries, bimahs, synagogue bathrooms and communal rooms, and Jewish school buildings accessible to people who use wheelchairs.

Our youngest children can help examine their synagogue and Jewish school buildings to see if there are Braille signs, wheelchair ramps, and clear sound systems. Older kids can take on some projects themselves; for example they can earmark tzedakah money to help buy large print books for the library and Braille prayer books or a better sound system for the synagogue. Our teens can volunteer to tutor children with learning problems and/or to record books on tape for people with visual disabilities.

We can also help our children recognize the role that language plays in showing kavod by encouraging them to use "people-first language" when they talk about individuals with disabilities. We can help kids of all ages understand which of the following descriptions of the same woman shows honor and respect: "There is a woman in a red dress eating ice cream," or "A crippled woman is eating ice cream."

The rabbis also teach that the concept of lo titeyn mikhshol (not to place a stumbling block) should guide our interactions with a person who is blind about a certain matter. Thus we need to teach our children that it is disrespectful to pretend to give good advice, while taking advantage of another's naïveté or ignorance. And we must help children see that differences among people should be respected. We can teach even young children not to tease those who eat, drink, or behave differently from the norm; there might be significant medical or emotional reasons for these behaviors that our kids don't understand. We can help our older children meet the responsibility of respecting their peers as people, even if they do not agree with their behavior or their beliefs.

HONORING ANIMALS: *TZA'AR BA'LEI CHAYYIM*

Judaism teaches us to honor all of God's creatures, not just the human ones. In Proverbs (12:10) we read, "A righteous person knows the needs of his beast." The mitzvah of tza'ar ba'lei chayyim—which literally means "the pain of living creatures"—deals with the appropriate treatment of animals. Our tradition teaches us to care for the animals that are our responsibility and that we are permitted to use animals for human benefit, provided we do not cause them unnecessary pain and suffering.

There are many laws in the Torah about the appropriate treatment of animals. Farmers plowing their fields are forbidden to harness a donkey and an ox together (Deuteronomy 22:10). These animals are not equally strong and it would be cruel to force them to work together. A farmer is forbidden to muzzle an ox that is working in the field, as would be unkind not to allow the animal to graze freely while it worked (Deuteronomy 25:4). And even beasts of burden should be permitted to rest on Shabbat (Deuteronomy 5:14).

More apropos to our modern lives, Judaism provides specific ways we can teach children to observe this mitzvah. The Talmud tells us that we are prohibited from buying an animal unless we can care for it. We can share this practical advice with our children when deciding whether to allow them to have a pet. We should teach our children that we are obligated to feed our animals before taking food for ourselves (*Berachot* 40a) and that we are permitted to perform acts normally forbidden on Shabbat to relieve an animal's suffering (*Shabbat* 128b). All children are capable of providing some care for a pet. We can help our young children to fill a pet's bowl with water or dry food. And by reminding our kids to do this, especially before they sit down to eat their own meal, we teach kindness and conscientiousness. Our older and more mature children can take on more responsibility for a pet, such as cleaning a cage, taking a dog for a walk, and providing kind and gentle attention.

There is a traditional Jewish belief that God intended people to be vegetarians. In the Garden of Eden, Adam and Eve were told to eat fruits and plants (Genesis 1:29). Only after the Flood did God give permission to eat meat (Genesis 9:3). The Book of Isaiah describes a future world in which no living creature will eat any other. If we choose to eat meat, Judaism mandates that we take the lives of animals in the most humane way possible. This is one of the purposes of the laws of *kashrut,* the dietary rules that determine whether something is kosher (fit or proper) for a Jew to eat. Whether or not our family eats meat or keeps kosher, we should help our children understand that Jews traditionally observed these laws to show honor and respect for the animals that provided their sustenance.

In light of this mitzvah, our children may ask us how it can be permissible to use animals for medical research. We can tell them that the prevailing Jewish opinion seems to be that animals may be used in research that might lead to a cure and/or prevention of human disease. This is *pikuach nefesh,* the mitzvah of saving a life.

PROTECTING THE EARTH: *BAL TASHCHIT*

When we teach our children to honor all of God's creations, we should remember to include respect for the earth itself. Jewish tradition teaches that the earth belongs to God and we are only its caretakers. In Psalms (24:1), we read, "The earth is the Lord's and all that it holds, the world and all its inhabitants." The mitzvah of *bal tashchit,* explains our responsibility to care for the earth. It is derived from Deuteronomy (20:19–20), which forbids cutting down trees that yield food, even during wartime. It is a "threshold" mitzvah, one that we can use to introduce our children to the idea of honoring the world and all that is in it.

Judaism teaches many practical ways of caring for the environment. "Care should be taken so that pieces of broken glass are not scattered on public land where they could injure people" (Babylonian Talmud, *Bava Kamma* 30a). "Whoever breaks dishes, tears clothes, demolishes a building, stops up a fountain, or uses food in a destructive way transgresses the law of *bal tashchit*" (*Mishneh Torah, Melakhim* 6:10). "It is forbidden to destroy animals" (Babylonian Talmud, *Chullin* 7b). "It is forbidden to make the oil in a lamp burn too quickly wasting fuel" (Babylonian Talmud, *Shabbat* 67b). Here we have Jewish support for energy efficiency, controlling pollution, preserving endangered species of plants and animals, and not littering. We parents can model these activities and encourage our children to participate with us.

We help our young children learn to respect the earth when we teach them to take bottles to the recycling bin, to turn off the water while brushing their teeth, and to turn out the lights when they leave a room. Kids of any age can be taught not to waste food. Our school-age children can help donate clothing and toys to a thrift shop, instead of simply throwing these items in the trash. And we can help our kids understand that through these acts they are not only helping the environment, by not adding to the local dump, but are also showing respect and honor for those who are less fortunate than they are. We can help our teenagers get involved with an environmental group, whether it is local or global. When we raise children who respect the earth and everything on it, they will naturally find many ways to honor God's creations.

TEACHING HONOR AND RESPECT

When practicing the middah of kavod, we parents look at ourselves and our relationships with our family, friends, and the world through a Jewish lens. We can thus help our children on the road to mensch-lichkeit, teaching them specific ways of living life more fully as menschen. We and our children can develop the best of our impulses into actions that honor God, ourselves, and one another. In doing so, we in turn become more honorable.

Judaism teaches us to honor all people, simply because they are created *b'tzelem Elokeim*, in the image of God. Our children should understand that respect is crucial to all human interactions; it is what makes people want to relate to others in a mensch-like way. Our children learn that when they demonstrate kavod to others, they are likely to receive kavod in turn, a formula that generates positive human relations. However, before we can expect our kids to honor other people, we must first help them respect themselves. We can begin a discussion of kavod by asking our children what makes them feel respected and who and what they respect and why. We can also help them identify behaviors that they feel demonstrate respect.

Taking Care of One's Own Body

Judaism teaches that part of honoring oneself is maintaining one's health and well-being. Our bodies are gifts from God and we should take joy and pleasure in them. When we teach these ideas to our kids, they will, we hope, want to avoid high-risk behaviors that hurt their bodies and engage in appropriate activities that will keep them sound and fit. We can begin to discuss kavod with our kids by asking them these kinds of questions:

- How do you honor your body?
- Can you think of any high-risk behaviors that you have to avoid?

The Doctor and the Farmer (a Talmudic Tale)

Once, when Rabbi Ishmael and Rabbi Akiva were walking in the streets of Jerusalem they met a sick man who asked them how to become well. They told him what medicines to take.

Then the man said, "Who made me sick?"

"God," the rabbis answered.

"Then why do you interfere with God's work? If God made me sick, why do you presume to make me well?" the man said.

The rabbis then asked the man what work he did. He said that he was a farmer. Then, the rabbis said, "Why do you interfere with God's work? Why do you cut the fruit off the vines and pick the vegetables from the ground?"

"If I don't work the land, it will produce nothing," the farmer said.

The rabbis said, "Don't you understand? Just as your plants and vineyards cannot grow without the care of a human hand, the body cannot remain healthy without care. Medicine is the manure and the doctor is the farmer who tills the ground."

Then the man understood, and he took the medicines and was cured.

- What did the farmer learn?
- Do you agree?
- Why do you take care of your body?

What Would You Do?

Preschool Children

Sally doesn't feel well; her throat and tummy hurt, her head aches, and she is very hot. It is almost time to go to Lisa's birthday party.

- What can Sally do?
- What do you think will happen?
- What might be a menschlich thing for Sally to do?
- What would you do?

ELEMENTARY-SCHOOL CHILDREN

Some of the girls in Jane's sixth-grade class are piercing each others' ears. Jane isn't sure what she should do.

- What are some things that Jane can do?
- What might happen if she does each of these things?
- How does your Judaism help you decide what to do?
- What do you think you would do?

ADOLESCENTS

Roger's basketball teammates have decided to get the team mascot tattooed on their arms. Jack tells them that it won't hurt and he knows a safe place to do it. Roger isn't sure what to do.

- What are Roger's options?
- What are the consequences of each option?
- What does Judaism suggest we do?
- How would you handle this?

Honoring Your Father and Mother

Judaism considers honoring our parents so significant that it is rewarded both in this world and in the World to Come. It is one of the few mitzvot with a promise attached to it, reinforcing its importance. We can teach our kids that the fifth commandment is a bridge between our responsibility to God and our responsibility to other people. We can open a discussion with these types of questions:

- What is your responsibility to your parents?
- How do you show them respect?

The Clever Wife (a Story from the Diaspora)

Once there was a king who said that he would only marry a woman who was willing to break off all relations with her parents after the wedding and never see them again. There were many women who wanted to be queen and were willing to do this. He held a contest and chose a wife. But after the wedding, the king was away from the palace on business so much that his wife died of loneliness.

The king mourned her, and then held a contest to choose a new wife. The same thing happened.

Finally, there was a beautiful young girl, an only child, who decided to enter the contest to become queen. Her parents were very unhappy because everyone knew of the king's rule for his wife. But the girl told her parents that she loved them and promised that she would see them again. She was so beautiful, kind, and good that the king picked her to be his wife.

Soon, however, the king began to travel and ignore her just as he had his other wives. The clever girl made a large doll, dressed it in man's clothing, and painted a face on it. When she was lonely, she talked to it, telling it all of her feelings.

The king soon wondered why his new wife was adjusting so well to life in the palace. He thought that she might be betraying him by having her parents visit. One night, he hid behind the curtains and heard her talking to her doll. He burst into the room and plunged his dagger into the doll. Blood flowed from the doll onto the floor.

"What is this?" the king cried.

"This is my sorrow and my grief," the queen answered. "If I had not told this doll all that was in my heart, I would have burst from my suffering."

Then, the king realized how cruel he had been. He was sorry for his hard heartedness and invited his wife's parents to visit her at the palace. The girl kept her promise to her parents that she would see them again.

☍

- What do you think of the king's rule?
- What did the girl teach the king?

What Would You Do?

PRESCHOOL CHILDREN

It's almost Mother's Day and Dan wants to do something special for his mom.

- What can Dan do?
- What do you think will happen?
- What might be a menschlich thing for Dan to do?
- What would you do?

ELEMENTARY-SCHOOL CHILDREN

Rena's parents are divorced and don't get along with each other at all. She has the lead part in the school show and wants both of her parents to be there.

- What are some things that Rena can do?
- What might happen if she does each of these things?
- How does your Judaism help you decide what to do?
- What do you think you would do?

ADOLESCENTS

Nancy loves her mother, but it seems that recently they are always fighting. Nancy doesn't want to hurt her mother, but she thinks her mother is kind of old-fashioned and resents it when her mother makes comments about her clothes, friends, dating, and school.

- What are Nancy's options?
- What are the consequences of each option?

- What does Judaism suggest we do?
- How would you handle this?

Honoring the Elderly

Our tradition teaches that we should honor the elderly for their wisdom and experience. We can help our children show respect to all older people, those who are sick and well, related to them and not. We can ask our kids the following questions:

- Why do you think that Judaism considers this to be so important?
- How can you show respect to elderly people?

The Sleeping Grandfather (a Traditional Story)

Once there was a man who had a precious diamond to sell. His elderly grandfather was asleep in the room where the diamond was kept. A jeweler came to buy the diamond and was in a big hurry. He wanted to see the diamond immediately and take it with him if he decided to buy it. The man who owned the diamond wanted to sell it quickly, but he didn't want to disturb his grandfather. The jeweler said that he couldn't wait and would go on to the next merchant, but the man still refused to disturb his sleeping grandfather.

As soon as the jeweler left, the grandfather woke up. The man quickly took the diamond and ran after the jeweler. The jeweler waited for the man, bought the diamond, and said that he was impressed that the man was willing to lose the sale of the diamond to avoid disturbing his grandfather.

- What do you think of the man's actions?
- What would you have done if you were this man?

What Would You Do?

Preschool Children

Brittany wants to go to her best friend's birthday party. There is a big family birthday party for her grandmother at almost the same time. Her friend will be mad at her if she misses her party and Brittany's grandmother will be hurt if she misses that party.

- What can Brittany do?
- What do you think will happen?
- What might be a menschlich thing for Brittany to do?
- What would you do?

Elementary-School Children

Avi's grandfather is sick and lives in an apartment building for senior citizens. Avi's parents want him to go with them to visit his grandfather every Sunday. Sometimes Avi gets invited to a friend's house. Besides, some Sundays his grandfather doesn't even know who he is.

- What are some things that Avi can do?
- What might happen if he does each of these things?
- How does your Judaism help you decide what to do?
- What do you think you would do?

Adolescents

Allison's grandmother fell and broke her hip. She can't live alone any longer, and Allison's parents want her to live with them. The only place for her to sleep is in Allison's bedroom, and her grandmother doesn't like Allison's music, posters, or television and is disturbed when Allison talks on the phone.

- What are Allison's options?
- What are the consequences of each option?
- What does Judaism suggest we do?
- How would you handle this?

Honoring Teachers

Judaism maintains that showing honor to teachers is almost as important as showing respect to God. Teachers, coaches, librarians, advisers, counselors, and principals all have critical roles to play in our children's lives. We need to help our kids see that these jobs are difficult and that these adults should be respected, even when our children disagree with them. We can help our children understand these concepts by asking them:

- Why do you think it is important to respect teachers and coaches?
- Do you know of times when people haven't shown respect to teachers and coaches?
- How do you show respect to teachers and coaches?

The Radish (a Hasidic Tale)

Rabbi Zev Wolf of Zbarazh always kept his door open to strangers, and many came to sit and learn from his holy teaching. The Third Meal of Shabbat was a favorite time for people to come. His followers were careful to speak only in soft voices so that they didn't disturb him when he was deep in thought.

Once, a poor and unlearned man came in and sat down at the table. He took out a large radish, cut it into pieces, and began eating with loud crunching noises. The rabbi's followers yelled at him, "Boor! How can you bring such bad manners to this holy table?" The man blushed with shame.

The rabbi looked up from his studies, sighed, and said, "How I would love a delicious radish right now. Does anyone have one?"

The man was filled with joy. He jumped up and gave the rabbi a piece of his radish, which the rabbi ate with great pleasure.

- Do you think the poor man was showing disrespect when he began eating?
- What did the rabbi's action teach his followers?

What Would You Do?

PRESCHOOL CHILDREN

Greg has two teachers in his class. He likes Mrs. Schwartz a lot, but doesn't like Mrs. Rappaport very much. At Hanukkah, everyone gives the teachers presents. Greg wants to give Mrs. Schwartz something special, but isn't sure what to do for Mrs. Rappaport.

• What can Greg do?
• What do you think will happen?
• What might be a menschlich thing for Greg to do?
• What would you do?

ELEMENTARY-SCHOOL CHILDREN

The coach of Rich's soccer team always seems to play the same kids and leave other kids sitting on the bench. Rich is the star forward so he gets to play, but his friend Jacob hardly plays at all. Rich doesn't think it's fair, but he doesn't want the coach to get angry at him.

• What are some things that Rich can do?
• What might happen if he does each of these things?
• How does your Judaism help you decide what to do?
• What do you think you would do?

ADOLESCENTS

Hilary's science teacher flunked the entire class on a major test and refused to give a makeup test or a chance to earn extra credit. Hilary and her friends studied hard and think that the teacher didn't ask fair questions on the test.

• What are Hilary's options?
• What are the consequences of each option?

- What does Judaism suggest we do?
- How would you handle this?

Cleaving to Friends

Most of us like to have friends. We need to help our kids see that friendship works both ways, that if they are honest, respectful, and caring of others, they will receive the same treatment from their friends. We can open a discussion of friendship with our children by asking these kinds of questions:

- What qualities do you want in a friend?
- What do you expect from a friend?
- How do you act toward your friends?
- Are you a good friend?

The Bail (a Story from the Diaspora)

Once there were two friends who loved each other dearly. After a time, circumstances forced one of them to move to a different country, but they promised to visit one another often. It happened that, while the friend who had moved away was visiting his friend, war broke out between their countries. The visiting friend was arrested as a spy and sentenced to death. He asked the king's permission to return home first to arrange things for his wife and children.

The king laughed and said, "Why should I let you go? You won't come back for your own funeral."

Then, his friend came forward and said, "I will go to prison in his place. If he doesn't return, I will die in his place." The king agreed to this plan.

On the morning of the day set for the execution, the man still had not returned. They took his friend to the gallows and prepared to hang him. Just then, the man appeared and demanded that he be hanged instead of his friend. The friend, who already had the noose around his neck, refused. They argued back and forth, each insisting that he be the one to die instead of his friend.

Finally, the king called for silence. "What an extraordinary friendship this is," he said. "I pardon you both. I have only one request: I want you both to be my friends, for friends such as you are as precious as gold." The three remained friends for the rest of their lives.

• What would you do to help a friend?
• What wouldn't you do to help a friend?

What Would You Do?

PRESCHOOL CHILDREN

Joanne's best friend, Lisa, wants to borrow Joanne's favorite cassette. The last time Lisa borrowed something, she broke it.

• What can Joanne do?
• What do you think will happen?
• What is a menschlich thing for Joanne to do?
• What would you do?

ELEMENTARY-SCHOOL CHILDREN

Jeff worked very hard to finish his all of his homework. His best friend, Mark, says that he didn't have time to finish math because he was doing his spelling. He wants to copy Jeff's math so that he won't lose points for having incomplete homework.

• What are some things that Jeff can do?
• What might happen if he does each of these things?
• How does your Judaism help you decide what to do?
• What do you think you would do?

ADOLESCENTS

Marla knows that her best friend, Kathy, is hoping that Jacob will ask her out. Marla also knows that Jacob doesn't want to ask Kathy out because he thinks she is too loud and talkative.

• What are Marla's options?

- What are the consequences of each option?
- What does Judaism suggest we do?
- How would you handle this?

Honoring All People

Judaism teaches us to honor all people because we are all created in the image of God. We should teach our children to respect the most vulnerable members of our society and those who are different from them. If we ask the following types of questions, our kids can begin to learn this mitzvah:

- How do you show people respect?
- What opportunity have you had to get to know someone with a physical, mental, or emotional disability?
- How to you show that person respect?

The Tramp (a Story of Elijah)

When Rabbi Meir was young, he pleaded with his father to teach him how to meet Elijah the Prophet. His father said that if he studied Torah with all his heart, he would meet Elijah. Meir studied for four weeks, and returned to his father and complained that he had not yet met Elijah. His father scolded him for his impatience and told him to continue studying.

One night, a tramp came to the house of study while Meir was there. Meir looked at the man in disgust for he was dirty and his clothes were ragged. Meir was angry to be interrupted while he was studying and he sent the man away.

The next day, Meir's father came to the house of study and asked him if he had met Elijah yet. Meir said no.

"Did no one come here last night?" his father asked.

"Just a dirty old tramp," Meir answered.

"And did you greet him and wish him shalom?" asked the father.

"No," Meir said.

"Well, you missed your opportunity," Meir's father said. "That was

Elijah the Prophet." And from that day on, Meir wished every stranger he met shalom and treated him with kindness.

- Why did Elijah the Prophet come dressed as a tramp?
- What lesson did Meir learn?

What Would You Do?

PRESCHOOL CHILDREN

A new boy comes to Jamie's school. He has braces on his legs and uses a wheelchair. Jamie wants to be friendly but he isn't sure how to play with the new boy.

- What can Jamie do?
- What do you think will happen?
- What might be a menschlich thing for Jamie to do?
- What would you do?

ELEMENTARY-SCHOOL CHILDREN

Elena's friend Jill has always been overweight, and she has started bringing salads and fruit for lunch. One of the girls offers Jill chips and a piece of pizza, but Jill wants only her salad. Some of the girls start teasing Jill about her "rabbit food."

- What are some things that Elena can do?
- What might happen if she does each of these things?
- How does your Judaism help you decide what to do?
- What do you think you would do?

ADOLESCENTS

Samantha's synagogue has a beautiful building, but the *bimah* is not wheelchair accessible. She hears that there are renovations planned for the sanctuary and knows that the synagogue has a big fund-raising drive to raise money for the project. When she sees a picture of the new sanctuary, she notices that nothing has been planned to change the *bimah*.

- What are Samantha's options?
- What are the consequences of each option?
- What does Judaism suggest we do?
- How would you handle this?

Honoring Animals

Judaism teaches that it is important to honor all of God's creatures, not only the human ones. We can teach our children that whether we keep animals as pets or use animals for food, for research, or to help us work, we have an obligation to treat them in a way that doesn't cause them unnecessary pain and suffering. To help our children learn to respect animals, we can ask them these types of questions:

- Why do you think Judaism cares about respecting animals?
- How do you show your respect for animals?

The Spider (a Story of King David)

One day, when David was in his garden he noticed a spiderweb. He said, "How beautiful is your world, Lord. But of what use is the spider who weaves things that no one wears?"

God answered David, "One day, you will need this creature and you will understand why it was created."

One day not long after, King Saul, who was jealous of David, decided to kill him. David ran away into the desert and hid in a cave. Saul's men came looking for David and started to search the caves. David heard the footsteps of Saul's soldiers just outside the cave where he was hiding. Then he heard a voice.

"There is no need to search this cave," the soldier said. "There is an unbroken spiderweb covering the door. Surely no one has come here in several days." The soldiers left without searching the cave.

David was saved from certain death. From that time on, he never questioned God's wisdom in creating any creature on the earth.

- Are there any creatures on earth that make you wonder why they were created?
- Does every creature have to have a purpose?

What Would You Do?

PRESCHOOL CHILDREN

Jordan wants a puppy for Hanukkah, but his parents say that he has to be able to help take care of it.

- What can Jordan do?
- What do you think will happen?
- What might be a menschlich thing for Jordan to do?
- What would you do?

ELEMENTARY-SCHOOL CHILDREN

Adam learns about being a vegetarian and decides not to eat meat anymore. Some of his friends try to convince him to eat hot dogs and hamburgers with them.

- What are some things that Adam can do?
- What might happen if he does each of these things?
- How does your Judaism help you decide what to do?
- What do you think you would do?

ADOLESCENTS

Shelby has read several articles about animals used for research on a variety of diseases. She is very concerned about the treatment of these animals, yet she understands why animal research is important.

- What are some of Shelby's options?

- What are the consequences of each option?
- What does Judaism suggest we do?
- How would you handle this?

Protecting the Earth

Caring for the environment is extremely important in Jewish tradition, since we are caretakers of the earth that God has given us. Our children can learn that it is our responsibility to preserve the earth for future generations. We can ask our children:

- What things do you do to avoid harming or destroying our environment?
- What do you do to help make the environment better for the future?

Honi and the Carob Tree (a Talmudic Tale)

Once, when Honi was out walking, he came upon a man planting a carob tree. He asked the man how long it would be until the tree would bear fruit. "Seventy years," the man answered.

"How do you know that you will be alive in seventy years?" Honi asked.

"Just as I found carob trees when I came into the world," answered the man, "so I am now planting carob trees for my children to enjoy."

- What do you think that Honi learned from this man?
- Why is it important to plant trees and do other things for the earth when we won't see the results for so many years?

What Would You Do?

PRESCHOOL CHILDREN

Jeremy gave his dad a plant for Father's Day. His dad doesn't have much time to water it, but Jeremy really enjoys helping take care of it and is learning what to do to keep the plant healthy.

- What can Jeremy do?
- What do you think will happen?
- What might be a menschlich thing Jeremy can do?
- What would you do?

ELEMENTARY-SCHOOL CHILDREN

Amanda's synagogue doesn't recycle. She sees people throwing bottles and cans in with the regular trash. She has learned that recycling is something that can make a difference. She also wants to suggest that the synagogue turn off the decorative lights at night and save power that way.

- What are some things that Amanda can do?
- What might happen if she does each of these things?
- How does your Judaism help you decide what to do?
- What do you think you would do?

ADOLESCENTS

Brad just got his driver's license and wants to drive to school. His parents think it's a waste of money and energy since he can take the school bus. Very few juniors and seniors take the bus and Brad doesn't want to either.

- What are Brad's options?
- What are the consequences of each option?
- What does Judaism suggest we do?
- How would you handle this?

Living with Honor and Respect

There is much about the world and the people in it to honor. We parents should help our children think about people as being created in the image of God, and in this way it will be natural for them to feel respect for others. When we instill respectful feelings in our children, they are likely to want to demonstrate that respect. And when they do, they will find that others respect them in turn. We can show our kids that these interactions are part of the foundation of menschlich behavior. If we parents show kavod to our friends, family, strangers, and the world, our children will learn by example. If we encourage our kids to show respect and honor, they will begin to think and behave in a more mensch-like way.

4

But He Hit Me First: Keeping the Peace

Shun evil and do good, love peace and pursue it.
—Psalms 34:15

S halom (peace) is both a greeting and a farewell. It is the way in which we should approach others and the way in which we hope to leave them. It is the beginning and ending of all of our inter-actions. The desire for shalom permeates our siddur (prayer book), and infuses our prayers. Of the Torah it is said, "Her ways are pleas-ant ways, and all her paths, peaceful" (Proverbs 3:17). Jews are taught not only to love peace but to search for it, in our relationships with friends, with the world, and deep within ourselves.

The three-letter root word in Hebrew for shalom is *shin-lamed-mem,* meaning "whole" or "completeness." This definition informs our understanding of the Jewish concept of peace. We begin by feeling whole and complete—at peace—with ourselves. Recognizing our strengths and weaknesses, we know who we are and what we want from the world and are comfortable with ourselves. Approaching life with positive energy, we accept life's challenges and attempt to meet them with grace and determination. We look at our glass of life as half full rather than half empty.

When we feel this peacefulness within ourselves, we are able to act peacefully toward others, treating them kindly, gently, respectfully, and lovingly. Judaism teaches that we must actively seek peace; it doesn't just happen. Peacefulness is a mindful way of engaging family, friends, and colleagues. It takes work, but is a process worthy of concerted effort. When we engage others in peace, we hope that they will return peacefulness to us. Although we may fail, we must continue to try. Moreover, the process of peace making improves us.

Within every Jewish prayer service is a plea to God to bless the world and all of its people with peace. We understand that peace is the greatest blessing of all, and believe it emanates directly from God. *Sim Shalom,* a prayer for peace, says:

> *Establish peace, well-being, blessing, grace, loving kindness,*
> *and mercy upon us and upon all Israel, Thy people.*
> *Bless us, our Parent, all of us as one, by the light of Thy Presence,*
> *For by the light of Thy Presence have You given us,*
> *O Lord our God,*
> *A Torah of life, love of kindness, justice, blessing,*
> *compassion, life, and peace*
> *And it is good in Thy sight to bless Thy people Israel at all times*
> *and in every hour with Thy peace.*
> *Blessed are You, Lord, Who blesses Your people Israel with peace.*
> (*Kol Haneshamah,* Wyncote, PA: The Reconstructionist Press, 1994)

We conclude the *Kaddish,* recited at the end of every service, and the Blessing after Meals with the request, "May God Who makes peace in the heavens, make peace for us and for all Israel." And in some congregations, the prayer ends with "and for all the peoples of world." Thus we acknowledge the importance of peace to us, as Jews, as citizens of the world, and as human beings. Our Torah is a living document of peace. Ours is a God of peace. And we are people of peace who pray for peace for all people .

HOW DO OUR CHILDREN LEARN SHALOM?

Our children begin to learn middot and mitzvot when they live them every day. It is the same with shalom. When we surround our young children with soft words and calm demeanors and create a peaceful and tranquil world for them, they feel peaceful, expect peacefulness, and radiate their own inner peace to others. And always, as our children grow, they take their cues from our behavior. When they see us at peace with others—refusing to participate in or even listen to gossip, being careful not to embarrass someone, and apologizing and making amends for our errors—our children learn to emulate our behavior.

If, on the other hand, we allow violence—in word or deed—within our home, our children will accept it in themselves and expect it from others. If we engage in screaming, arguing, and sarcasm, so will our kids. Our children learn about interpersonal relationships by what they see at home. If we hit our children, they will hit others. If we insult our children or others, ours will insult people, too.

Yet life is full of conflict, and as children grow older they should learn from us what to do when all is not peaceful, when problems arise. We parents must help them acknowledge conflict, express it with dignity, and apologize when necessary. The problem-solving and conflict-management techniques our children learn from us and practice within the home serve them well as they learn to get along with friends, teammates, and co-workers. And, as always, it is important for us to model these techniques and discuss them with our kids.

When we are faced with a relationship problem that we can solve peacefully, we should explain to our children that we are practicing the middah of shalom, grounding our actions in a Jewish context. One way of helping our children discover peaceful ways to solve their problems is to role-play challenging situations. Then when such problems arise, we can encourage our children to view them as opportunities to enlist their newly developing interpersonal skills.

THE PEACE THAT DWELLS WITHIN

Peace is often defined by what it isn't: war, fighting, acrimony. Yet peace is much more than that. We must help our children see that personal peace and internal harmony are the basis from which peace between people and nations begin. And we need to help them learn that achieving peace within themselves is an active and ongoing process.

Sh'lomo ibn Gabirol, an eleventh-century philosopher, said, "He is the greatest of men whose mind is most tranquil and whose association with others is most happy" (*Mivhar Hapeninim* 400). How do we and our children achieve that elusive feeling of *shalem,* of being whole, complete? There are probably as many answers as there are people searching for inner peace. For some of us, peace is a result of our relationship with God. In Psalms (4:9) we read, "Safe and sound, I lie down and sleep, for You alone, O Lord, keep me secure." Others of us find our peace in meditation, song, dance, writing, yoga, or tai chi. We can find peace by taking long walks, swimming, or gardening. Each of us needs to feel our way gradually, through trial and error, to explore our inner selves. When we model these methods of achieving peacefulness and tranquility, our children learn to pursue their own internal peace.

Our tradition gives us an opportunity for finding inner peace— Shabbat. Our weekly day of rest provides the respite we need from our usual pursuits so that we can release our minds and souls. No matter how traditional or how modern our practice, we can all find some time on Shabbat to step away from our daily pressures. By putting aside this special time each week, we send a clear message to our children, especially if we spend this precious time with them. The internal peace we achieve spills over and affects our dealings with the world. Martin Buber wrote, "When people have made peace within themselves they will be able to make peace in the whole world" (*Tales of the Hasidim: The Later Masters*).

PEACE IN THE WORLD

Peace throughout the world is an elusive goal that people of good will have been striving to achieve since the dawn of time. From the moment that Cain struck down Abel, brothers and nations have been fighting. How then are we, and our children, to create peace in the world?

First, we must accept God's answer to Cain's question (Genesis 4:9), "Am I my brother's keeper?" Rabbi Joseph Telushkin, in *Jewish Literacy*, wrote, "In essence, the entire Bible is written as an affirmative response to this question." Thus peace in the world becomes the responsibility of every one of us, each in our own small way. We must be willing to do our part to begin creating shalom, even though we will not be able to complete this work. Our tradition teaches, "It is not incumbent upon you to finish the job, but neither are you free to desist from it" (*Pirke Avot* 2:20). When we try to make the world a little bit better, a little more pleasant and peaceful, whether by smiling at a person we pass in the street or by holding the door for the person behind us, we are contributing toward *shalom b'olam*, peace in the world.

We must help our children adopt a global view. We Americans no longer have the luxury of feeling isolated from events that happen in other countries. We need to teach our children to understand and care about people whose names we can't pronounce or whose customs are decidedly different from our own. All people everywhere are our neighbors; what affects them must matter to us.

We can encourage our older children to read newspapers and magazines and to watch news programs to learn about world events. We should engage them in dialogue, sharing our opinions and questions with them. We can support our children's participation in their school's student government, in model United Nations programs, and other activities that teach them about peace between people and among nations. And even our youngest children can participate with the household in tzedakah projects on a global level, demonstrating with our actions that we are responsible for others, no matter who or where they are. The lessons we teach our children about peace will help create a more peaceful world.

AN ACTIVE PROCESS

Judaism teaches that peace does not just magically descend on us. Although we pray for peace, this alone is insufficient. Peace is the end result of an active and highly personal process, and this is reflected in the words we use: to "make" peace and to "pursue" peace. We have to do something to create peacefulness.

Yehiel ben Yekutiel, in his *Sefer Maalot Hamiddot,* wrote:

> Seek peace with your friend and pursue it with your enemy. Seek it in your place and pursue it in other places. Seek it with your body and pursue it with your money. Seek it for yourself and pursue it for others. Seek it today and pursue it tomorrow. And do not despair, saying, "I will never achieve peace," but pursue it until you do.

In other words, we must work for peace and not give up. It may cost us time, energy, and money, but both inner peace and peace among people are worth our efforts.

It is truly important—and demanding—to model peacefulness for our children. When the schoolyard bully or the class gossip works their nasty business, our children may not feel much like making peace. And sometimes the peace-making tactics they try fail. It is difficult for us to continue to encourage our kids to stay on this challenging path. It is often tempting and all too human to want to fight back, with words if not with fists. Yet, our children are better served when we help them seek alternative solutions.

MITZVOT

There are many ways that we can teach our children to pursue peace. From the time they are small, children can learn to live peacefully within themselves, with family and friends, and with the world. The mitzvot that help us live peacefully make life more pleasant for us, as they make us more pleasant people. These are mitzvot that children of all ages and stages of development can understand and live out.

KEEPING PEACE IN THE FAMILY: *SHALOM BAYIT*

Our children's earliest learning environment—their *bayit* (home)— is the first place they learn about and experience peaceful behavior. And it is the first place in which they have the opportunity to create peacefulness for others. Although some of us may take our home and family for granted, putting on our company behavior only for friends and strangers, Judaism extols the virtues of beginning our mitzvot at home. Rabbi Simeon ben Gamaliel said, "Scripture esteems the person who makes peace in his house as if he made peace for every person in Israel. But Scripture demeans one who brings jealousy and strife into his house as if he had infected the whole House of Israel" (*Avot de-Rabbi Natan* 28:3). And Proverbs (17:1) tells us: "Better a dry crust with peace than a house full of feasting with strife."

We can find a clue about how to begin creating our own *shalom bayit* in the words of Rabbi Adda bar Ahavah. When his disciples asked him, "To what do you attribute your long life?" he replied, "I have never lost my temper in the midst of my family" (*Ta'anit* 20b). Of course, we parents are only human, and we do get angry at times, even at our beloved children. To teach our children peace, we must work to control our own tempers. We must not let anger take over our actions. Instead, we must remember that our ultimate goal is shalom. We must be especially careful never to strike out—physically or verbally—at our children. When we are angry, we must try to find a way to move past it and to work together with our children to find an answer to the problem.

As in all aspects of ethical behavior, we parents are the ultimate example for our children. When we show them that we can manage our anger while acknowledging our feelings, our kids learn to deal peacefully with others. We can help our children control their own anger by teaching them to take a time-out, to count to ten, or to practice deep breathing. When we model self-control, our children will follow suit.

Another important part of teaching our children to create a peaceful home is encouraging them to find ways to help out their parents and siblings. Rabbi Phil Warmflash, director of the Jewish Outreach Partnership in Philadelphia, says that even when his children do something as commonplace as setting the table for dinner, he explains to them that they are "helping to make the family more complete and we call this *shalom bayit*." When we label our children's daily actions a mitzvah, we lift those actions out of the ordinary, and our kids will learn that they can make a difference.

An important aspect of creating shalom within the household is to encourage our children to get along with their brothers and sisters. Although sibling rivalry is as old as Cain and Abel, we parents must help our youngsters interact with tolerance and cooperation, patience and generosity of spirit. We can model active listening, anger management, and peaceful methods of problem solving. We must also guard against showing favoritism and must show each of our children that he or she is special. When we help our kids learn to share not only toys but also our attention, we help them learn how to move through their lives in peace.

MAKING PEACE AMONG PEOPLE:
HAVA'AT SHALOM BEN ADAM LEHAVERO

Our children all too quickly move out into the world and begin to relate to people of many different humors and temperaments. Even very young children interact with people of all ages who are not members of their family, whether in daycare or at swimming lessons. We give our children a gift when we help them learn how to live in peace with others as well as how to initiate peaceful behavior.

A story is told about Rabbi Meir. He used to say, "When two men quarreled, Aaron would sit with one and say, 'Do you know what so-and-so is doing? He berates himself for the spat and wonders how to face you, he is so ashamed he behaved so badly.' Aaron would sit until he removed all of the rancor from the man's heart. Then, he'd go and do the same with the other person. When the two met, they would embrace each other" (*Avot de-Rabbi Natan* 12). While we may not have the wisdom or influence of Aaron, Judaism teaches us to do what we can to create peaceful interactions among people. When our young children begin to play in groups, we parents need to guide them toward appropriate interpersonal behavior. Deborah Aaron, co-director of the Lieberman Jewish Family Life Education and Group Services of Jewish Family and Children's Service of Philadelphia, recalled to me that, when her children were little, there developed "a feeling like family among the children in the neighborhood." This feeling was enhanced by parents who clearly articulated the ethics of how their kids were to treat each other, saying things such as, "On this street, boys and girls play together."

Social issues can become fairly complex for our teenagers. Teens may find themselves called on to mediate disputes between friends. We can help them think of an explanation for one person's seemingly bad behavior or remember someone's redeeming qualities. If we have modeled peaceful behavior with our own friends, our teens may find a way to help their friends talk to each other openly and politely. This is a challenging task, but one that mature adolescents can handle.

Judaism teaches us a practical way to live in harmony with others: "Should people strive with you . . . make peace with them so that when you leave them they no longer speak angrily about you" (*Derekh Eretz Zuta* 9, 11). If our kids see that we never leave a person angry with us and that we soothe hurt feelings and apologize for misdeeds before parting, they will learn to become peacemakers. We can encourage this same behavior in our kids by teaching them to not end the day on an angry note. A quick phone call or e-mail to a friend can help save a relationship. If it is too late in the evening for our child to talk with his friend, we can help him make a plan to discuss differences of opinion, apologize, and/or make peace the following day. When we teach our children that the future good of a friendship or other relationship transcends the need to win every battle, they—and we—are ultimately the winners.

ACTING WITH COURTESY: *DEREKH ERETZ*

One sure way we make and maintain peaceful relations with others is when we treat them courteously. The manners and good breeding we teach our children never go out of style. Being polite goes a long way toward keeping the peace. Although manners are more relaxed and informal today than they were in the early twentieth century, civil and courteous behavior is still the menschlich thing to do.

Ben Zoma, in the Talmud, described courteous behavior this way: "What does a good guest say? 'How much trouble my host has gone to for me.' . . . What does a bad guest say? 'What kind of effort did my host make for me?' " (*Berachot* 58a), The difference is focus. When we are focused inward, on ourselves, we are not being courteous. But when we are focused outward, on others, we are able to recognize kindness and hospitality when it is offered.

We teach our young children this outward, other-directed focus by treating them courteously, so that they understand and appreciate how nice it feels. When they spontaneously respond in kind, we should reward them with praise and more courteous behavior. Even preschool children can be taught to speak politely. When we say "please," "thank you," "you're welcome," "excuse me," "bless you," "I'm sorry," and "no problem" we grease the gears of interpersonal relations. Children who hear these phrases regularly will likely use them often.

As our children mature, we should teach them social responsibilities such as prompt responses to invitations, written thank-you notes for gifts, and telephone etiquette—especially in this age of personal cell phones. Our children should be taught to greet guests courteously, by name and with a firm handshake. And we can help our children see that such behavior helps create more peaceful and kinder interactions between people. Family dinners are perfect opportunities for parents to model and teach polite table manners and appropriate conversation skills. Although our kids may never dine with royalty, we should prepare them so that they could.

Our children can learn that these social niceties are not outdated and that they still make sense in a world in which appearances and first impressions can mean a lot. When our children have mastered these skills, they will feel comfortable in any company and will be able to move easily into any adult situation they choose, contributing to their own inner peace and self-confidence. And although basic courtesies don't guarantee peaceful relationships, they certainly start things off on the right foot.

Being Slow to Anger: *Erech Apayim*

When we lose our temper, we temporarily abandon control of ourselves. And when we vent our feelings in a violent and/or hurtful way, others will treat us with anger as well. If we want to live in a peaceful world, we must first learn to live in peace ourselves.

Being slow to anger is first mentioned in the Torah as one of the attributes of God: "The Lord! the Lord! a God compassionate and gracious, slow to anger, abounding in kindness and faithfulness, extending kindness to the thousandth generation, forgiving iniquity, transgression, and sin" (Exodus 34:6–7). This does not say that God never becomes angry—there are many examples in the Torah of God's wrath. Nor does it imply that we should never get angry. It does, however, suggest that God-like behavior means maintaining control over our anger so that we do not hurt those around us.

We should teach our children to recognize and acknowledge their own anger, so they can learn appropriate expressions of their feelings. If we encourage our kids to keep their feelings bottled up, never permitting them to express a negative emotion, then we are setting them up to explode someday and to say and do things they will regret.

Noah Ben Shea, in *The Word: A Spiritual Sourcebook,* described the Gastiner Rebbe's way to handle anger. Whenever he was offended or took offense at something someone said to him, on that day he would never say anything to the person about how he felt. Instead, he would let his emotions rest and would sleep on the matter. The next day, he would approach the offender and say, "I was not happy with you yesterday." His technique included both a cooling off period (like counting to ten or taking a time-out) and the direct, but gentle, expression of his true feelings. Even if the person did not change his behavior, the Rebbe could feel satisfied with his own behavior. We can share this story with our children and use it to discuss ways of controlling anger. The story also demonstrates that self-restraint comes from a place of strength, not weakness.

Yitzchak Buxbaum, in *Jewish Spiritual Practices,* relates another method for keeping the peace by being slow to anger: Rabbi Hayim Yosef David Zucai said, "If someone you are with is provoking you to anger, be silent; if you have to speak make it a point to speak in a low and gentle voice as this will keep anger from overcoming you. This is a good device to see that an argument that starts does not continue and get larger." When our school-age children are having difficulty with their tempers, we can encourage them to try this method. By responding in a calm way, they will help keep the peace.

We can teach our older children to write down their feelings and the events that caused them. Sometimes this helps them gain clarity and understanding while distancing themselves from the immediacy of their feelings. This method may enable our teens to confront the object of their anger in a productive fashion.

GUARDING YOUR TONGUE: *SHEMIRAT HALESHON*

The Talmud tells a story about Rabbi Gamliel, who sent a servant out to buy the best and the worst foods in the market. When he returned, the rabbi asked the servant to show him the worst food. The man opened a basket and showed the tongue of an ox. Then, the rabbi asked his servant to show him the best food. Again, the servant opened the basket and showed the rabbi the tongue of an ox. "Why," the rabbi asked, "have you brought the same food when I asked you to bring the best and the worst food in the market?" The servant replied, "There is nothing worse than a tongue when it speaks only *lashon harah* [evil speech], and nothing better than a tongue when it speaks words of wisdom and kindness."

We can use this story to teach our children that speech is one of the most significant aspects of our humanity. We can show them that one of the best ways to behave in a mensch-like manner and to pursue shalom is to guard their tongues, using the gift of speech only for good. The strength of our words is reflected in Proverbs (18:21)— "Death and life are in the power of the tongue"—and in Ben Sira (28:18)—"Many have fallen by the sword, but more by the tongue." Our children should understand that they can do a great deal of good or a great deal of harm through what may seem like merely a few simple words.

Our tradition teaches that it is a mitzvah to avoid three categories of "evil" speech. Even our young children can understand these concepts on some level and be encouraged to keep the peace by not engaging in such talk. The first category, *lashon ha-rah* (the evil tongue), includes making unfavorable, damaging, or false comments about someone or something. Our children should understand that sharing ethnic jokes, spreading negative gossip or rumors, or even telling a true story that places a person in a bad light are all harmful.

The second category, *motzi shem ra* (giving someone a bad name), includes even inadvertently spreading gossip that is untrue. Children of any age can learn that they should not repeat negative stories, especially since they cannot be sure that such stories are even true. They can also learn not to embarrass or humiliate someone deliberately, even a person they dislike, by telling lies. Exodus (23:1) teaches, "Do not carry rumors that are untrue." The final category, *rechilut,* involves telling our friends the negative gossip about them that we heard from someone else. Even young children can see that nothing is gained by reporting such gossip—except hurt feelings and disruption of the peace. One of the most important lessons we can give our kids is to help them see that they cannot know the ultimate outcome of such unfavorable speech. As the Talmud says, "What is spoken in Rome may kill in Syria" (Genesis *Rabbah* 98:23).

Sometimes children cannot imagine what harm can be caused by engaging in gossip, especially if the story seems funny to them. But Judaism believes that "the gossiper destroys three people: himself, the listener, and the victim" (*Arakhin* 15b). We parents must show our children that a community in which gossip is common is a community in which people cannot truly live together in peace.

Our children will learn to guard their tongues if we carefully guard our own. If we do not engage in gossip and refrain from making unkind comments about others, our kids will also learn to live this mitzvah. It is important, as always, to discuss these issues with children, teaching them to see the more subtle instances of speaking with an "evil" tongue. If we, too, are struggling with this issue, we can ask our children to help us see our own transgressions. In this way, we can learn to keep the peace together.

On the other hand, we must make it clear to our kids that they can come to us to discuss the events and upsets of their day. And, if in such intimate sharing, they must say something negative about someone else, we must not discourage it. We can point out that such talk can be tolerated when we are seeking advice for ourselves or to better offer help to a friend.

Being Careful Not to Embarrass: *Lo Levayesh*

We parents can teach our children another practical way to live in peace: Avoid placing people in embarrassing situations. Shaming and humiliating others can cause lifelong enmity. We wound the very spirit of the victim, which is often a wound that is harder to heal than one of the flesh. The Talmud tells us the seriousness of embarrassing someone with words: "One who publicly shames a neighbor is as though that person shed blood. . . . One who whitens a friend's face in public has no share in the World To Come." (*Bava Metzi'a* 58b–59a).

As parents, we must remember that adults who think nothing of embarrassing others were often themselves humiliated as children—by parents, teachers, or peers. One way to break this cycle and to help our children have peaceful relationships with others is to realize the pain our own words can cause. Sometimes we use pet names for our children, without thinking about how *they* feel about those names. When we call our shy child "little mouse" or our husky child "my baby elephant," we can cause lifelong pain and embarrassment. When we are sarcastic to our kids or humiliate them—even in "fun," we should not be surprised when they are hurt. And because our children imitate what we do and say, we cannot be surprised when they have difficulty maintaining friendships.

It is critical that we teach our children not to embarrass others. And so we must begin with our own behavior, carefully watching how we talk to our kids, friends, and family. By the time our kids enter school they are old enough to know what it feels like to be embarrassed. We can encourage them to first think about how they would feel before they say something that might embarrass a classmate. Rabbi Jacob Staub, vice president for academic affairs of the Reconstructionist Rabbinical College, noted that if one of his children was caught embarrassing someone, a sincere apology was essential and the lesson was reinforced with a donation to the family tzedakah box.

FOREGOING REVENGE: *LO TIKOM*

"I only hit him back," is a favorite plaint of children, usually cried from the backseat of the car on long road trips. It is of utmost importance that we help our children learn to forego revenge. Many of the world's wars have been fueled by the notion that if someone else did something bad first we are entitled, even obligated, to hurt back and take retribution. It is often difficult for our kids to trust that they can contribute to keeping the peace simply by refusing to hit back. Yet, it is a mitzvah to forego revenge. In Leviticus (19:18) we are commanded, "You shall not take vengeance or bear a grudge against your countrymen." And our tradition teaches us that before hitting back, we should say to ourselves: "Just because this one is petty and malicious, should I follow suit? Rather let me behave graciously toward the person who will realize it and thus increase harmony and love" (*Biur* to Leviticus 19:18).

Maimonides took this idea a step further, teaching that it is a mitzvah not to bear a grudge: "As long as one nurses a grievance and keeps it in mind, the person may come to take vengeance" (*Yad Hazakah*, Deuteronomy 7:8). Thus we must help our children learn to let bad feelings go rather than storing them up. We can teach them to reach out a hand in peace and friendship rather than a fist in anger. In this way, they can offer an opportunity for peace instead of conflict. The Rabbis explained what this means:

> What is revenge and what is bearing a grudge? If A says to B, "Lend me your sickle," and B says, "No," and the next day B says to A, "Lend me your ax," and A replies "I will not, just as you refused to lend me your sickle," that is revenge (and is forbidden by the Torah). And what is bearing a grudge? If A says to B, "Lend me your ax," and B says "No," and the next day B says to A, "Lend me your garment," and A replies, "Here it is. I am not like you, who would not lend me what I asked for," that is bearing a grudge. (*Yoma* 23a)

Not hitting back is an exercise in self-restraint that is difficult for many of us to achieve, let alone teach to our children. On the surface, it seems fair to strike back, figuratively if not literally, when we have been struck. And it seems somehow justified, at the very least, to remind others that we did not strike back and thus are much more righteous than they. How, then, do we teach the mitzvah of *lo tikom* to our children?

Foregoing revenge is another "threshold" mitzvah—one that we can use to teach our children how to live in peace with others. Yet our younger children may not have the maturity to control their impulses and our older kids may not fully understand the difference between showing restraint and being a coward. One thing we can do is to explain our actions in terms of this mitzvah and our Jewish traditions and writings. We can also back up our stance with stories of people such as Gandhi and Martin Luther King Jr., who courageously used nonviolence to achieve great things.

MAKING AMENDS: *TESHUVAH*

The word *teshuvah* brings to mind Yom Kippur, our yearly exercise in making amends for all of our sins. All of us make mistakes; that is part of what it means to be human. "Teshuvah" comes from the Hebrew word that means "to return," and when we apologize and make amends we turn away from things that have hurt others and return to the menschlich path of peace. We also find a "turning," a change, within ourselves, as we face our faults and promise ourselves, and others, to do better in the future.

If we truly wish our children to live in peace with their fellow human beings—an important characteristic for a mensch—we must show them that once a year is not often enough to express regret for actions that cause others pain. Because our children mirror our behavior, we must do our best on a daily basis to take stock of our actions, correct our misdeeds when possible, apologize to those we have injured, and try not to repeat our mistakes. Judaism teaches that this is what God and other people want from us.

Maimonides outlined a four-step process for making amends that we can teach our children even in today's world. First, we must help our children recognize when they have done wrong. "One must know his deeds. . . . If one does not know wherein he has transgressed, how can he regret what he has done?" (*Orchot Tzaddikim*) When we are open and secure enough to admit when we have gone astray, our children will feel comfortable doing the same.

Second, we must help our children truly regret what they have done. We can teach our children that complete and sincere regret, promptly expressed, plays a large part in whether their apology is believable and, ultimately, acceptable. And we should teach our kids that only when they honestly regret their actions can they take the third step: changing their future behavior. We parents can help our children understand that mistakes offer them a chance to better themselves. When we help our children see the positive aspects of their mistakes, they will learn from them.

The last step is to encourage our children to ask forgiveness from the person they have harmed and to offer compensation for any damage they have done. We should let our kids know that we understand how much courage this takes. If we support and love our children, they should have the strength to take this step. For our youngest children, it may be enough for them to say they are sorry directly to the person they hurt. But our teens can go further, facing the consequences of their actions. Proverbs (28:13) reminds us that "He who covers up his faults will not succeed; He who confesses and gives them up will find mercy."

We can begin to teach this mitzvah when we show our children that we ourselves go through all four steps when we make mistakes. Modeling this behavior and discussing our actions with our children will give them the courage to practice teshuvah themselves.

TEACHING PEACE

When we pursue the middah of shalom, we are pursuing menschlichkeit. We are, indeed, fully human when we live in peace with ourselves and with others. From our children's earliest days, we should make them a peaceful home and help them find peace among their family and friends. From the base we give them, our kids, in turn, become conduits of peace in the world, practicing and actively pursuing shalom within themselves and among all the people who come into their lives. It is reassuring to know that there are positive steps we can take to help our children live peacefully in the world.

Talk
About It

The Jewish concept of peace is much more than simply the absence of war. Shalom comes from a feeling of completeness within ourselves, which allows us to feel inner peace. When we help our children feel this inner peace, they are more likely to approach others peacefully. And we, as their parents and primary teachers, can help our children discover the tools to work toward both types of peace. We can start a discussion about shalom by helping our children figure out the things that make them feel peaceful toward others. From there, we can talk about how they feel when they are not at peace with themselves or their friends. Together, we can identify the types of behavior that promote peaceful relationships and those behaviors that hinder them.

Keeping Peace in the Family

The first place that our children learn about living peacefully is in their own home. We can create an environment in which we all feel more peaceful toward one another and behave in a peaceful manner. We can open a discussion with our children by asking these kinds of questions:

- Is our home a peaceful place?
- What would we need to do to make it more peaceful?

Spitting in the Rabbi's Eye (a Talmudic Tale)

Once there was a woman who went to synagogue every Sabbath to hear Rabbi Meir teach, for his words made her feel very good. One day, the rabbi's talk lasted longer than usual and her husband came home to find the house empty. He became very angry that she was not there to greet him and serve his dinner, and he vowed that she could not return to the house again until she had spit in the rabbi's eye.

"I could never do such a shameful thing," the woman said. She went to stay with her parents and think about what to do. Rabbi Meir heard what had happened. He sent for the woman and when she arrived he told her that he had something in his eye. "I heard," the rabbi said, "that such a pain can be eased if a good woman spits into the eye seven times." The woman protested and said that she could not do such a thing, but Rabbi Meir insisted. So, in front of the rabbi's students, the woman spat seven times into the rabbi's eye. Then, the rabbi said, "Go and tell your husband that you spat into my eye not once, but seven times."

The woman went home. Her husband, who realized that his jealousy and bad temper were wrong, apologized to her. After she left, Rabbi Meir's students asked him how he could have permitted such an indignity. "But there was no indignity," the rabbi answered. "There can be no disgrace in doing something that brings peace to a household."

- Do you agree with Rabbi Meir?
- What usually causes problems in your family?
- What can you do to help the members of your family live peacefully together?
- How do you feel when you do something to help create *shalom bayit*?

What Would You Do?

Preschool Children

Bonnie is watching her favorite program on TV. Her little sister comes in and starts to jump and dance in front of the television.

- What can Bonnie do?
- What do you think will happen?

- What might be a menschlich thing for Bonnie to do?
- What would you do?

ELEMENTARY-SCHOOL CHILDREN

Zach and his brother Adam have matching soccer shirts. Zach can't find his, even though he knows he left it over a chair in his room. Adam comes into the kitchen wearing a soccer shirt that Zach is pretty sure is his, because he remembers that Adam spilled juice on his own shirt at the last game.

- What are some things that Zach can do?
- What might happen if he does each of these things?
- How does your Judaism help you decide what to do?
- What do you think you would do?

ADOLESCENTS

Debbie wants to go shopping for a prom dress. She would prefer to go with her two best friends, but she knows that her mom, who loves to shop, has been waiting for this opportunity. Debbie doesn't want to hurt her mom's feelings, but she really wants to go with her friends.

- What are Debbie's options?
- What are the consequences of each option?
- What does Judaism suggest we do?
- How would you handle this?

Making Peace among People

When our kids move out into the world, their ability to live in peace with others may be sorely tested. Whether they are involved in a dispute with someone or are the mediator between friends, it is important that they learn how to make peace with people who are not always sure how to live peacefully. We can help our children understand how to make a peaceful world by asking questions like these:

- Why is it our job to be peacemakers?
- What can you do to live peacefully with others that doesn't make you feel that your own rights have been denied?
- What can you do to help your friends live peacefully with one another?

A Share in the World to Come (a Talmudic Tale)

One day, Rabbi Beroka Hoza'ah was walking through the marketplace with the prophet Elijah, who used to appear to him in the disguise of a beggar. The rabbi asked Elijah, "Do you see anyone who has a share in the World to Come?"

Elijah looked around, and then pointed to a man. "That man," he said.

The rabbi ran after the man and when he caught up with him said, "Tell me, sir, what is your occupation?"

"I am a jailer," the man replied.

Rabbi Beroka wondered why this man would have a share in the World to Come and asked, "What exactly do you do?"

"I make certain that the people in the jail do not hurt one another," the man answered.

"I see," the rabbi said, understanding now why the man had a place in the World to Come. Then Rabbi Beroka turned to Elijah and asked if there were any other people in the marketplace who had a share in the World to Come. Elijah looked around again and pointed to two other men. Rabbi Beroka walked up to them and asked them what they did.

"We are jesters," they replied.

"Jesters?" the rabbi said, wondering why they deserved a place in the World to Come.

"Yes," the men replied. "We delight in cheering people up when they are depressed. And, if we should see two people quarreling, we bring them laughter and make peace between them."

Then Rabbi Beroka smiled to himself. He understood why the prophet Elijah said that each of these people would have a place in the World to Come.

- Why do you think each of these people has a place in the World to Come?
- What do you do when friends of yours are quarreling?
- What responsibility do you have to be a peacemaker or to try to prevent people from hurting one another?

What Would You Do?

PRESCHOOL CHILDREN

Arielle is playing in the yard with her best friend, Rachel. Rachel keeps the swing until it is almost time to go in for dinner. Arielle is very angry with Rachel and doesn't want to play with her anymore.

- What can Arielle do?
- What do you think will happen?
- What might be a menschlich thing for Arielle to do?
- What would you do?

ELEMENTARY-SCHOOL CHILDREN

Noah sees that his buddies Mike and Ted are getting ready to argue about the video game the three of them have been playing. Every time they play together, Mike and Ted argue. Each one is sure that he knows the best way to play. This really ruins it for Noah.

- What are some things that Noah can do?
- What might happen if he does each of these things?
- How does your Judaism help you decide what to do?
- What do you think you would do?

ADOLESCENTS

Suzanne knows that her two best friends, Becca and Emily, like Mark. Mark has been dating Becca but is breaking up with her to go out with Emily. Becca is hurt and angry because she thinks that Emily has been flirting with him. Suzanne is worried about how this will affect the friendship of the three girls.

- What are Suzanne's options?
- What are the consequences of each option?
- What does Judaism suggest we do?
- How would you handle this?

Acting with Courtesy

We can teach our children that treating other people courteously is a good starting place for living peacefully with them. Our kids should learn to treat others as they would like to be treated, one of the keys to being a mensch. We can help our children understand the importance of courtesy by asking them the following types of questions:

- What do you do to act courteously toward other people?
- How do you feel when you act this way?
- How do you feel when other people are courteous to you?

The Importance of a Greeting (a Story from the Holocaust)

There was a Hasidic rabbi who lived in Danzig before World War II. Every morning he would take a walk. He was careful to fulfill Rabbi Yoḥanan's advice and would greet everyone he met with a warm smile and a cordial "Good morning." Over the years, the rabbi got to know many of the townspeople and would always greet them by name.

In the field near the town there was a farmer. The rabbi used to pass him each day, and would always greet him, saying "Good morning, Herr Muller."

"Good morning, Herr Rabbi," the man would answer.

When World War II started, the rabbi's walks ended. He lost his entire family at the Treblinka death camp and was later taken to Auschwitz. Herr Muller had joined the Nazi SS. One day, there was a selection at Auschwitz and all of the Jewish inmates had to pass in front of a Nazi officer who signaled some people to go to the left, which led to the gas chambers, and others to the right, which led to a life of slave labor.

As the line moved forward, the rabbi thought he recognized the voice of the person sending people to the right or to the left. Soon, he could see the man's face. As he came in front of the man, the rabbi heard himself saying, "Good morning, Herr Muller."

"Good morning, Herr Rabbi," the man responded. "What are you doing here?"

The rabbi smiled faintly and said nothing. Herr Muller lifted his baton and signaled the rabbi to go the right, to life. He was later transferred to a safer camp and survived the war. After the war, the rabbi told this story about his life and said, "This is the power of a good morning greeting. A man must always greet his fellow man."

- Why do you think courteous behavior is important?
- Can you think of any times that your courteous behavior has made a difference in your life?

What Would You Do?

PRESCHOOL CHILDREN

Abby and her mom are taking the train home from shopping in town. It is very crowded and there aren't enough seats. Abby's mom is standing and tells Abby to give up her seat to an old lady. Abby is tired and really wants to sit down.

- What can Abby do?
- What do you think will happen?
- What might be a menschlich thing for Abby to do?
- What would you do?

ELEMENTARY-SCHOOL CHILDREN

Robbie's parents taught him to shake hands when he meets someone, stand when an older person comes into the room, and give up his seat on the bus for an older person. If he does these things when he's with his friends, they tease him.

- What are some things that Robbie can do?
- What might happen if he does each of these things?
- How does your Judaism help you decide what to do?
- What do you think you would do?

ADOLESCENTS

Jessica is in English class, and there is a substitute teacher. Several kids are throwing spitballs, calling out, and being generally rude and obnoxious. It makes Jessica uncomfortable.

- What are Jessica's options?
- What are the consequences of each option?
- What does Judaism suggest we do?
- How would you handle this?

Being Slow to Anger

Most people lose their temper at some point. Yet an important mitzvah is to be slow to anger. We teach our children that they are more likely to behave peacefully toward other people when they learn to control their temper. When we ask the following types of questions, we help our children live this mitzvah:

- What makes you lose your temper?
- Do you have any strategies for controlling your temper?

Rabbi Hillel's Temper (a Talmudic Tale)

Rabbi Hillel was known to be patient and slow to anger. Once, two men made a bet that they could make the great rabbi angry. One of the men declared that he knew just what to do. He went to Hillel's house just as the rabbi was making preparations for the Sabbath.

Instead of greeting Hillel politely, the man was as rude as possible and called out that he was looking for Hillel. The great rabbi went out to greet him and politely asked what he could do for the man. The man, thinking the rabbi would lose his temper over a ridiculous and impolite question, said, "Tell me why the heads of Babylonians like you are so round." Hillel did not grow angry. Instead, he answered the man seriously, and said, "You have asked a good question. Babylonians' heads are round because they do not have good midwives to help women give birth."

The man left, but soon returned and again called for Hillel. He said that he had another question to ask. Hillel calmly told him to ask his question. "Why are the Palmyreans so bleary eyed?" the man asked.

Hillel remained calm and told the man that this was another good question. "The answer is that the Palmyreans live in the desert and the wind is always blowing sand into their eyes," he answered.

Again the man left, only to return in a few minutes with another rude and ridiculous question for the great rabbi. "Why are the Africans' feet so wide?" he asked.

Hillel did not get angry and told the man that again he had asked a good question. "The answer is that the Africans live among watery marshes and their wide feet allow them to stand."

Finally, the man said, "I have many more questions, but I am afraid you will become angry if I ask them of you."

At that, Hillel sat down with the man and said, "Please ask all the questions you want."

Then the man said, "May there be no other like you in all Israel. Because of you, I have lost my bet of four hundred zuz."

"Be careful of your moods, my son," the great rabbi said. "The fact that I have not grown angry may be worth your money. And no matter how much money it would cost you, I would still not lose my temper. You see, the price of anger is greater than any amount of money."

- Why do you think Hillel did not get angry with the man?
- Why is the price of anger greater than money?
- When has getting angry ever cost you something?

What Would You Do?

PRESCHOOL CHILDREN

When Ann and her little sister, Katie, play together, Katie leaves a mess and sometimes breaks things.

• What can Ann do?
• What do you think will happen?
• What might be a menschlich thing for Ann to do?
• What would you do?

ELEMENTARY-SCHOOL CHILDREN

Stewart thinks that Tim is not doing his share of the work on their history project. It is due next week. and Tim has just said that he can't work on it after school. Stewart really wants to get a good grade on this project, so he has been doing extra work all along.

• What are some things that Stewart can do?
• What might happen if he does each of these things?
• How does your Judaism help you decide what to do?
• What do you think you would do?

ADOLESCENTS

Gail took Joyce's history book out of her locker when she couldn't find her own. She didn't return it, and Joyce needs it to study for a test. This isn't the first time that Gail has borrowed something and not returned it. And she always seems to do it just when Joyce needs the borrowed item.

• What are Joyce's options?
• What are the consequences of each option?
• What does Judaism suggest we do?
• How would you handle this?

Guarding Your Tongue

Words are important; they can affect how we think about things and how we behave. We teach our children that speaking negatively about someone is a sure way to anger and hurt that person. And we help our kids understand that speaking positively whenever possible—or not making a negative comment—will help them maintain peaceful relationships. We can open a discussion of this mitzvah by asking these kinds of questions:

- Are you careful about what you say to and about other people?
- Do you gossip about others or listen to other people gossip?
- How do you feel when you know that people are talking about you?

Gather the Feathers (a Folk Tale)

Once there was a man who disliked the rabbi of the town. He started to tell a story around town that he had seen the rabbi steal an apple in the marketplace. In truth, the shopkeeper had given the rabbi the apple. Everyone in town heard the story and wondered if their rabbi was a thief. Finally, the man realized that the story had spread all over the community, and he began to regret what he had done. He went to the rabbi and begged his forgiveness.

The rabbi replied that he would forgive the man on one condition. The man was to go home, take a feather pillow, cut it up, and scatter the feathers to the wind. The man did as the rabbi had said, and then returned to the rabbi and asked to be forgiven.

"Just one more thing," the rabbi said. "Now, go and gather up all the feathers."

"But that's impossible," the man said. "The wind has already scattered them."

"Just so," the rabbi replied. "And just as you truly wish to correct the evil you have done, it is as impossible to repair the damage your words have caused as it is to gather up the feathers."

- Why is it impossible to correct the evil that gossip has caused?
- Have you ever hurt someone with your words?
- What did you do about it?

What Would You Do?

PRESCHOOL CHILDREN

Jack called Sarah a nasty name, and she doesn't like him. To get even, Sarah wants to tell her mother that Jack took money from the tzedakah box.

- What can Sarah do?
- What do you think will happen?
- What might be a menschlich thing for Sarah to do?
- What would you do?

ELEMENTARY-SCHOOL CHILDREN

George hears Jason and Ryan talking about Sam. George is a good friend of Sam's and wants to help him if kids are talking about him.

- What are some things that George can do?
- What might happen if he does each of these things?
- How does your Judaism help you decide what to do?
- What do you think you would do?

ADOLESCENTS

Jacob and a bunch of his friends are standing around telling jokes they have gotten off the Internet. One of Jacob's friends starts telling a joke about Polish people that Jacob thinks is very offensive. All of the other guys are laughing and clearly think it's very funny.

- What are Jacob's options?
- What are the consequences of each option?
- What does Judaism suggest we do?
- How would you handle this?

Being Careful Not to Embarrass

Shaming and humiliating others can cause lifelong hatred because we remember the pain of our embarrassment long after the event itself. We need to help our kids see that it is sometimes possible to go out of our way to avoid shaming someone, which is a very powerful way to live in peace with others. We can teach our children about embarrassment by asking these types of questions:

- How do you feel when you are embarrassed?
- What could you do to avoid embarrassing others?

Bar Kamza's Honor
(a Story from the Second Commonwealth)

In Jerusalem, there lived a man who had a friend named Kamza and an enemy named Bar Kamza. The man gave a dinner party and sent his servant to invite his friend Kamza to the party. The servant made a mistake and brought Bar Kamza instead.

The man told Bar Kamza to leave. Bar Kamza was embarrassed and asked the man to let him stay. The man refused. Bar Kamza offered to pay for his food and drink. The man refused and loudly told him to leave. Then Bar Kamza offered to pay for half the party. Again, the host refused and yelled, "Get out of my house." Bar Kamza offered to pay for the entire cost of the party. At that, the host stormed over to Bar Kamza, pulled him to his feet, and pushed him out of the door and onto the street.

Bar Kamza was embarrassed and furious. "Not even the rabbis who were there tried to prevent my humiliation," he thought. "I will teach them all a lesson."

Bar Kamza went to the Romans and told them that the Jews were rebelling against Rome. To prove it, he told them to send a sacrifice and see if the Jews would offer it on the Temple altar. So the Roman governor selected a calf without a blemish and sent it with Bar Kamza. On the way, Bar Kamza made a small mark on the white of the calf's eye, which made it unacceptable for a Jewish sacrifice.

The rabbis wanted to offer it anyway so as not to offend Rome, but Zechariah ben Avkulus objected. "We can not set a precedent that it is permissible to offer animals with blemishes," he said. So, the people decided not to sacrifice the calf. Then they decided to kill Bar Kamza so that he would not tell the Romans what they had done. Again, Zechariah ben Avkulus objected. "We do not kill people simply because they blemish a sacrifice," he said.

The anger of Rome did come down on them: Jerusalem was destroyed, the Temple was burned, and the Jews were exiled from their land.

Rabbi Eliezer taught, "This shows how serious it is to embarrass a person. In order to defend Bar Kamza's honor, God was willing to destroy even the Holy Temple."

- Do you think that Bar Kamza was right to do what he did?
- Have you ever embarrassed someone?
- What was the result?

What Would You Do?

PRESCHOOL CHILDREN

There is one boy in Jared's play group who is fat and runs slower than everyone else. Some of the boys have started to call him "Fat Stuff" and "Slowpoke."

- What can Jared do?
- What do you think will happen?
- What might be a menschlich thing for Jared to do?
- What would you do?

ELEMENTARY-SCHOOL CHILDREN

Mark loves baseball and tries hard in every game. Miriam doesn't like Mark and she knows that Mark will be embarrassed if she says something in front of his friends about his striking out twice in the championship baseball game.

- What are some things that Miriam can do?
- What might happen if she does each of these things?

- How does your Judaism help you decide what to do?
- What do you think you would do?

ADOLESCENTS

David knows that Abe likes Lauren and is trying to impress her. He also knows that Abe is very sensitive about his acne. Some of the other guys are teasing Abe about it when Lauren walks by.

- What are David's options?
- What are the consequences of each option?
- What does Judaism suggest we do?
- How would you handle this?

Foregoing Revenge

When someone does something bad to us it is natural to feel that we want to get even or take revenge. We help our children make giant strides toward living in peace if we teach them to forego revenge. We can begin a discussion of this difficult concept by asking our children the following types of questions:

- Have you ever made the conscious decision not to take revenge on someone who hurt you?
- Why did you make that decision?
- How did you feel?

The Vengeful Aunt (a Hasidic Tale)

Once, the Baal Shem Tov and his disciples went on a trip to Berlin. When they arrived, they heard that a young bride had just died on the evening before her wedding. When the groom heard that the Baal Shem Tov had arrived in his town he came to ask the Baal Shem Tov to intercede with heaven on their behalf. The Baal Shem Tov told the groom to wrap the bride in her shroud and take her to the cemetery. He said to lay her and all her wedding garments in the grave, but not to cover her.

The groom did as he was told. Then the Baal Shem Tov stood above the grave and looked down at the lifeless bride. His own face drained of color and his body went stiff. Suddenly, the young woman's cheeks flushed with color and she sat up. "Put on her veil and bring her to the wedding canopy at once," the great rabbi said.

The Baal Shem Tov performed the wedding and then left. Then the bride told her story. "Once, my husband was married to my aunt. When she realized she was about to die, she became jealous of me and thought that my uncle would marry me when she was gone. She made us swear never to marry each other. But after she died, we did fall in love and eventually we decided we must marry. Last night, my aunt returned from the dead to take revenge on us for breaking our vow. The Baal Shem Tov interceded in heaven and demanded that she give up her claim on us. The Heavenly Court ruled in our favor."

Then the happy couple and all of their friends rejoiced at the wedding feast.

- Why do you think the Heavenly Court ruled in favor of the couple?
- What do you do when someone has hurt you?

What Would You Do?

PRESCHOOL CHILDREN

Eric and Joey are in the backseat of the car. They have a bag of books to share on their family's vacation. Joey doesn't see any books that he wants except the one that Eric just took, so Joey pulls Eric's book away.

- What can Eric do?
- What do you think will happen?
- What might be a menschlich thing for Eric to do?
- What would you do?

ELEMENTARY-SCHOOL CHILDREN

Leah knows that Jillian told a bunch of their friends that Leah cheated to get an A on a math test. It isn't true, and Leah is very angry. Leah saw Jillian's test paper and knows that she got a D on the test.

- What are some things that Leah can do?
- What might happen if she does each of these things?
- How does your Judaism help you decide what to do?
- What do you think you would do?

ADOLESCENTS

Nancy's sister, Janet, refused to lend Nancy a sweater to wear to a school dance. Nancy was angry, but found another sweater. Now, Janet wants to borrow Nancy's leather jacket to wear on a date.

- What are Nancy's options?
- What are the consequences of each option?
- What does Judaism suggest you do?
- How would you handle this?

Making Amends

Despite all of our good intentions, we make mistakes, do things we know we shouldn't do, hurt other people, and generally make a mess of things. When this happens to our kids, we should teach them that the best thing they can do at that point is make amends. We can help our kids realize what they have done, take responsibility for it, correct their mistakes and misdeeds, and apologize to those they have injured. Because we parents understand that this is difficult, we must support our children and help them see that teshuvah is an important step toward rebuilding a peaceful relationship. To talk to our children about making amends, we can start by asking these questions:

- Have you ever had to apologize for something you did?
- How did you feel before you apologized?
- How did you feel afterward?

The Mirror and the Glass (a Hasidic Tale)

Once Rabbi Eisig traveled to a village where only one poor Jew lived. The poor man took him in, fed him, and prepared a bed for him. Yet the man was sad because he couldn't show the rabbi the honor the rabbi deserved. The rabbi was so touched by the man's distress that he gave him his blessing before he left.

From then on, the man's fortunes changed, and he soon became very wealthy. He was so rich that many beggars came to his door, and he hired a guard to send them away. He soon became cruel and heartless.

Some time later, Rabbi Eisig returned to the village and went to visit his former host. This time, the guard started to turn him away. Rabbi Eisig said, "Tell your master that I am the one responsible for all his wealth." The guard soon returned with permission for the rabbi to enter. It was obvious, however, that the man was eager for the rabbi to leave.

"Look through that window. What do you see?" Rabbi Eisig asked.

"People going about their business," the man replied.

"Now look in this mirror. What do you see?" the rabbi said.

"Just myself," answered the man.

"Both the window and the mirror are made of glass. Through one you can see others, and through the other you can see only yourself. The only difference is the gilt coating. It is time to scratch off the gilt."

At that, the man understood what he was doing wrong. He made a true repentance and never again turned a poor person away from his door.

- What does a person need to do to show repentance to you?
- What have you had to do to show your repentance?

What Would You Do?

Preschool Children

By accident, Lonnie spilled paint all over Alan's picture. Alan had worked all afternoon on it, and he was very angry. Lonnie said that she was sorry, but Alan was still mad.

- What can Lonnie do?
- What do you think will happen?
- What might be a menschlich thing for Lonnie to do?
- What would you do?

ELEMENTARY-SCHOOL CHILDREN

Nurit asked Dahlia if she could borrow her CD player, and Dahlia said no. Nurit took it anyway. She dropped it on the way to school and it broke.

- What are some things that Nurit can do?
- What might happen if she does each of these things?
- How does your Judaism help you decide what to do?
- What do you think you would do?

ADOLESCENTS

Nathan told his parents that he would be home by midnight. He and his friends went to a movie and then out to eat afterward. He lost track of the time and was late getting home.

- What are Nathan's options?
- What are the consequences of each option?
- What does Judaism suggest we do?
- How would you handle this?

Living with Peace

When we try to live in peace with people we are truly behaving in a way that is menschlich. We must help our children learn that shalom spreads from them to others to the world and that they have the power to change the nature of everything they interact with. By encouraging our children to think about how good they feel when they are at peace with themselves and with others, we help them see how important it is to work toward creating a peaceful world.

5

Not-so-Random Acts of Kindness

The world couldn't exist for even one hour
without acts of kindness.
—Otiot Rabbi Akiva

*H*esed, lovingkindness, smoothes out the rough spots in the world. Along with Torah study and worshiping God, it is one of three pillars on which Jews believe the world stands (*Pirke Avot* 1:2). Although Jewish tradition considers certain specific actions to be deeds of lovingkindness, it is not the deeds alone that demonstrate hesed. The attitude with which the deed is performed is what makes a mundane act into something holy. The action alone is not enough; the feelings, whether implied or expressed, behind our acts are critical.

Hesed is expected of us because we are created *b'tzelem Elokeim*, in the image of God. Because God did acts of lovingkindness, we are obligated to do so ourselves (*Sotah* 14a). The Torah tells us that God clothed the naked (Genesis 3:21), visited the sick (Genesis 18:1), buried the dead (Deuteronomy 34:6), and comforted mourners (Genesis 25:11). And our rabbis and scholars have identified other acts of lovingkindness, such as welcoming guests, giving tzedakah, and feeding the hungry. Each act of lovingkindness requires us to give of ourselves—be it our time, energy, skill, or attention.

Although many of us freely give money to help those less fortunate than us, that act, in and of itself, is not sufficient. In the Talmud we read, "Our rabbis taught: Lovingkindness is greater than charity in three ways. Charity is done with one's money, while lovingkindness may be done with one's money or with one's person. Charity is given only to the poor, while lovingkindness may be given both to the poor and to the rich. Charity is given only to the living, while lovingkindness may be shown to both the living and the dead" (*Sukkot* 49b). Although some people do not need our money, all people need our lovingkindness.

Most of us find it easy to be kind and loving toward those we deem worthy. Yet Judaism teaches that we are to "act with kindness both with him who deserves it and with him who deserves it not" (Sh'lomo ibn Gabirol, *Mivhar Hapeninim*). And when we extend our kindness to all people, we in turn become deserving of lovingkindness. As with most mitzvot, the more we give, the more we receive.

When we teach our children hesed, they learn to respond to their best impulses. We must help kids think about how they would like others to treat them—and then encourage them to make the first move. Hesed requires that we put aside pettiness, selfishness, possessiveness, and miserliness and try to give our best to others. Even if our good deeds are not returned in kind, we are more fully human for trying to act in the image of God.

WHAT IS HESED?

The biblical mitzvot that God performed give us examples of the types of deeds that we can do to sweeten the lives and ease the burdens of our fellow human beings. These thoughtful acts let others know that we truly care about them. If we are sensitive to the lives and needs of the people we interact with, we will find an abundance of opportunities to give lovingkindness.

Lovingkindness is so important to human life that Jewish law does not quantify it (*Pe'ah* 1:1). Because our tradition does not specify an all-inclusive list of acts of lovingkindness or tell us how much time we must spend or how many acts we are obligated to perform, we must work from our hearts and not our heads. And this is exactly what turns an ordinary action into a deed of lovingkindness—we are kind to others with no thought of measuring or counting or looking for payback, benefit, or reward. When we perform an act of lovingkindness, it is because we have a desire to do good that arises from our love for God and God's creations. We show that we are grateful for what we have and that we wish to give something back to the world.

Deeds of lovingkindness can take many forms. Sometimes we help by giving money, and sometimes we do a greater good by helping people learn to help themselves. We perform acts of lovingkindness when we give someone something they need or something we think they might enjoy. But we also do good deeds when we offer our time, presence, advice, or expertise.

We should also remember that hesed—perhaps more than other middot—has as much to do with attitude as it does with action. We engage in acts of lovingkindness in a way that is loving and kind. We do not begrudge the time, effort, and money that we spend. The process is almost as important as the outcome.

Maimonides wrote, "Whoever gives charity to a poor man ill-manneredly and with down cast looks has lost all merit of his action even though he gives him a thousand gold pieces. He should give to him with good grace and joy and should sympathize with him in his plight. . . . He should speak to him words of consolation and sympathy" (*Mishneh Torah*, 10:4). A loving, empathic attitude may make it easier for the recipient to accept the kindness that is offered.

Most of us have, at times, performed an act of kindness routinely or even reluctantly. Before we are too harsh on ourselves, we should remember that our rote deeds may still be preferable to not acting at all. Better to feed a poor person than to let him starve. We hope that as we develop the habit of doing deeds of kindness, the loving feeling will follow.

A popular bumper stick exhorts us to "Commit random acts of lovingkindness." These acts are the little things that present themselves to us every day: we offer to help a colleague carry a package, we bring a friend a cup of coffee, or we take the neighbor's newspaper to her on a rainy day. All around us are opportunities to help make another person's life easier or simply more pleasant.

We can encourage our children to look for these opportunities as well. Maybe they can help a friend with school work, sharpen a classmate's pencil, offer to walk home with the new kid in the neighborhood, or invite a lonely child to join them at the lunch table.

We can also perform not-so-random acts of kindness. In the *Book of Jewish Values,* Rabbi Joseph Telushkin wisely suggests that we schedule kindness into our days. He recommends looking at our calendars and writing in a specific deed to be performed at a specific time. He explains this by quoting Rabbi Nachman of Bratslav: "If you're not going to be better tomorrow than you were today, then what need have you for tomorrow?"

HOW DO WE TEACH HESED?

We teach lovingkindness, we do other middot, by modeling such behavior for our children. When our children experience hesed and see us perform daily acts of lovingkindness, they will learn to do the same. Even our toddlers can engage in these deeds. At first, we may have to suggest age- and skill-appropriate acts—such as drawing a picture for a sick neighbor—but as our children mature, they will find their own ways to engage in lovingkindness.

Our school-age children and teens can help us when we do hesed. We can volunteer together at a nursing home or visit a sick friend or relative. Our kids can help us cook a meal for a neighbor who just came home from the hospital or can collect their outgrown clothes and unneeded toys to give to a shelter. And they can pitch in when we make preparations for welcoming a guest for Shabbat dinner or a seder. Once our children get in the habit, they will spontaneously think of ways to do hesed themselves and may, in fact, suggest things to us.

Many of us give monetary donations regularly to tzedakah. Parents should not assume our children know and understand what we are doing. Instead, we should make a point to discuss our actions with our kids, explaining how we decide the amount of money to give and where to give it. And when we allow our children to have a voice in determining where some of the family donation should go, they may surprise us with their thoughtful suggestions.

We should also encourage our children to give some of their own money to tzedakah. Our youngest kids can give their pennies, developing a habit that will last a lifetime. Our older children can give from their allowances or from money they've earned. It is important for us to teach our children the Jewish idea that "Charity is equal in importance to all the other commandments combined" (*Bava Batra* 9b).

One way we can teach our children about the great effect that acts of lovingkindness can have on others and the world is to tell them about people who made just such a difference. Danny Siegel, founder of the Ziv Tzedakah Fund, has written many books about "ordinary" people who have changed the world through their kind deeds. By sharing these stories with our kids, we can inspire them to perform hesed. We can make a tremendous impact on our children by helping them see the menschlich things that their friends, neighbors, relatives, teachers, and coaches do every day. In this way, our kids will learn that they, too, can make the world a better place.

The movie *Pay It Forward* celebrated the notion that we should take the first step and perform acts of lovingkindness for others— even for strangers—who have not done the same for us. And instead of having the recipient return the favor by helping us, that person should help someone else, thus paying the good deed "forward." If each person performed just three such acts, then soon everyone in the world would be engaged in hesed. The movie seems to focus on the very Jewish concept of spreading deeds of lovingkindness outward beyond one's own small circle of family and friends to the community and, ultimately, the world.

Many children participate in community service activities in their secular schools, but we should make them aware that hesed has been a Jewish tradition for thousands of years. As our kids enter Jewish adulthood, their preparation for their Bar and Bat Mitzvahs should include taking on a mitzvah project. We can encourage our young teens to plan a task in which their own efforts can make a difference. We can also suggest that our children donate a portion of the monetary gifts they receive to a tzedakah of their choice. As a family, we can earmark left over food for Mazon, a Jewish group that distributes it to shelters and other facilities, and can donate the flower arrangements to a hospital or nursing home. Older kids can even make such donations in person. With a little thought and ingenuity, we can help our children think of many other ways of doing hesed.

WHO DESERVES OUR GOOD DEEDS?

Jewish tradition teaches us that everyone deserves our good deeds. Because all people are created in God's image, all should be recipients of our kindness. Furthermore, we cannot judge whether people are deserving of hesed; only God can make such a judgment. Rabbi Telushkin, in *The Book of Jewish Values,* tells us that Rabbi Smelke of Nikolsberg said, "When a poor man asks you for aid, do not use his faults as an excuse for not helping him. For then God will look for your offenses and God is sure to find many."

We should remember that our goal is to look for opportunities to do deeds of lovingkindness, regardless of the recipient's actions. Rabbi Yoḥanan said, "Be always like a helmsman, on the lookout for good deeds" (Leviticus *Rabbah* 21:5). We should try to find more ways to give of ourselves and not evaluate and judge others, finding fewer ways. Rabbi Telushkin notes that Rebbe Chaim of Sanz said, "The merit of charity is so great that I am happy to give to one hundred beggars even if only one might actually be needy. Some people, however, act as if they are exempt from giving charity to one hundred beggars in the event that one might be a fraud."

We cannot know the ultimate effects of our loving gestures. But because each of our good deeds has the possibility to change a life or the world for the better, we may be the catalyst to spur someone else to perform hesed. If not, at least we are doing something positive for our own hearts and minds.

Our tradition teaches us that our first responsibility is to our family, community, and people. For who will help them if we do not? But then we should turn our attention outward, remembering that all people are created in God's image. The Talmud says: "We must provide help for the non-Jewish poor as well as for the Jewish poor; we must visit non-Jews when they are sick as well as our fellow Jews; and we must attend to the burial of their dead as well as the burial of our own dead" (*Gittin* 61a).

MITZVOT

Of the many mitzvot that are traditionally considered deeds of lovingkindness there are some that are especially appropriate to teach our children. When we model these mitzvot for our kids, we must remember that our intentions are as important as our actions.

WELCOMING GUESTS: *HAKHNASAT ORCHIM*

The Talmud says that offering hospitality to others is one of the pleasures enjoyed in this world and rewarded in the World to Come (*Shabbat* 127a). Welcoming guests can be as great a pleasure to us as it is to them. This mitzvah is not merely a duty but is a joy.

Among other things, Abraham is celebrated for his example of *hakhnasat orchim*, "bringing in guests" (Genesis 18:1–8). The Torah tells us how he went out to greet strangers who approached his tent, offered them his finest food and drink and a chance to rest in the shade, and even washed their feet for them. We learn the ideal way to perform this mitzvah from his example. He actively sought the opportunity to offer hospitality by keeping the sides of his tent open to watch for passersby and by running to greet them. He anticipated their needs and generously offered the best of what he had available. In our efforts to be like Abraham, we, too, should try to go beyond the minimum standard of courtesy, so our guests feel welcome and comfortable in our homes.

In biblical times, this mitzvah was so important that several other examples appear in the Torah. Lot, Abraham's nephew, offered hospitality to two angels who came to destroy the evil city of Sodom (Genesis 19:1–3). Abraham sent his servant Eliezer to Haran to find a wife for Isaac. There he met Rebecca, who included his animals in her offer of hospitality. From this act of lovingkindness, Eliezer knew that she was the woman he should select for Isaac. And, when Moses fled Egypt to Midian, he saved seven young women from a group of shepherds who were harassing them. Their father, Jethro, invited Moses to eat in his home, and he gave Moses his daughter Zipporah as a wife (Exodus 2:20).

Throughout Jewish history, it has remained important for Jews take care of one another by practicing this mitzvah. The Talmud attributed the destruction of the Second Temple to unnecessary hatred, epitomized by a lack of hospitality (*Gittin* 55b–56a). The Rabbis said that it was permissible, if necessary, to work on Shabbat to make room for guests (*Shabbat* 126b). Hospitality during Passover, a central theme of the seder, comes from Rabbi Huna's words: "Let all who are hungry come in and eat" (*Ta'anit* 20b). In the Middle Ages, some communities even established a committee, called the *Chevra Hachnasat Orchim,* to help visitors find meals and lodging. It was a privilege to invite yeshivah students home for a meal, and the custom of reciting *Kiddush,* the blessing over the wine, at the synagogue on Friday night was established so that visitors could bless and drink the Shabbat wine.

The mitzvah of welcoming guests is easy and fun to teach children. Most of us enjoy having guests and opening our homes to others. When we include our children in the planning and preparation, they will feel proud of our hospitality. We can ask our youngest children to pick up toys or magazines, so that the house looks nice. Older kids can help with cooking, cleaning, decorating the house, and making other preparations. When company arrives, children of all ages should be encouraged to visit briefly with and talk to the guests. In this way, our kids are able to participate in this mitzvah, practice their manners, and learn to be at ease with adults.

Our children should be free to offer the hospitality of their homes to their friends. We can encourage our kids to invite friends over to study, have band practice, have a party, or just hang out. Not only will our children be performing a mitzvah but we will have an opportunity to be involved and connected with our kids, their activities, and their friends.

We can also model this mitzvah for our children by making an effort to invite guests for Shabbat dinner, the seder, and other Jewish holidays. In almost every community we can find Jewish travelers, college students, new neighbors, or older people who have no family close by. We should make it a habit to ask our rabbi or Hillel director if they know of someone who would welcome such an invitation.

Not only should we teach our children the mitzvah of welcoming others into our home but we should make them aware of what it means for them to be a good guest in someone else's home. If our kids are used to helping us prepare for guests, then they should be reminded that their host has done the same for them. We can teach our children that one way to show their appreciation of their host's efforts is to have a small house gift with them when they arrive. And we should encourage our kids to help pick out that gift. We should also teach our children to write a thank-you note when they get home. No matter how short the visit, our children should know that they must be polite, helpful, adaptable, and easy to please.

FEEDING THE HUNGRY: *MA'AKHIL R'EVIM*

The story of Abraham welcoming the strangers to his tent also teaches us about the mitzvah of *ma'akhil r'evim*, feeding the hungry. When he prepared food and drink for his guests he gladly and willingly offered them the best that he had. His generous attitude made this a deed of lovingkindness. When we feed the hungry, we, too, should offer the best that we can, with an open heart.

The Torah provides guidance about how to carry out this mitzvah. We are instructed to leave fruit and grain in the fields for poor people, making it easy for someone who needs food to find it, without the added shame of having to ask: "When you reap the harvest of your land, you shall not reap all the way to the edges of your field, or gather the gleanings of your harvest. You shall not pick your vineyard bare, or gather the fallen fruit of your vineyard; you shall leave them for the poor and the stranger: I am the Lord your God" (Leviticus 19:9–10). Moreover, we should feed not only the members of our own community but also strangers. When we perform this mitzvah, we should extend our lovingkindness to poor and hungry people wherever and whoever they are.

Jews do not take having enough food for granted. The Torah commands us, "When you have eaten your fill, give thanks to the Lord your God for the good land which God has given you" (Deuteronomy 8:10). Thus we say the *Motzi* (blessing over bread) before each meal and the *Birkat ha-Mazon* (grace after meals) afterward, making the everyday act of eating into something holy. By doing so, we remind ourselves of the origin of the blessings we enjoy and raise our children's awareness of what it means to have sufficient food.

One way to teach our children the importance of feeding the hungry is to discuss with them how it would feel to be hungry or always to have to worry about where the next meal will come from. If we then perform the mitzvah of providing food to those who are hungry, our kids will better understand the connection between our gratitude for our own abundant food and the action that the mitzvah demands.

Jewish holidays, which usually seem to center around food, are wonderful times to model this mitzvah for our children. On Purim, it is traditional to give gifts of food to the poor, *mattanot le'evyonim*. We are supposed to give enough for a meal for two people. Children of any age can help collect canned and packaged goods for a shelter or can help us prepare and deliver a meal. It is traditional to invite guests to partake of our Passover seder, and we can ask our kids who they would like to invite. We can also encourage our children to contribute to our community's *Maot Hittim* (the gift of wheat), a special fund used to help purchase Passover food for people in need. And we can take our children along when we donate our *chametz* (leavened food that is not kosher for Passover) to the community food bank or other non-Jewish agency.

VISITING THE SICK: *BIKUR HOLIM*

Since at one time or another, we have all been sick, we know how important the loving concern of caring friends and family can be. The Talmud teaches, "Whoever visits a sick person helps the person to recover" (*Nedarim* 40a). Visiting a sick person is said to take away one sixtieth of the person's illness (*Nedarim* 39b). And Rabbi Akiva said that when we fail to fulfill this mitzvah we can be considered to have shed blood (*Nedarim* 40a).

The Talmud teaches that just as God visited the sick, so must we (*Sotah* 127a); by doing so, we mirror the merciful qualities of God. The Rabbis understood that such a gesture promotes good will between people. They therefore suggested that Jews should visit the sick, even if the patient is not Jewish (*Gittin* 61a). Moreover, Rava, a fourth-century rabbi, said that the mitzvah is not fulfilled with a single visit. If a patient requires more attention, one should visit him repeatedly.

The Rabbis also considered practical matters. They said that in the first three days of an illness only family members should visit (*Pe'ah* 3). The first and last hours of the day were not considered to be good times to visit (*Nedarim* 40a); according to Maimonides, these times were normally devoted to medical care (*Hilkhot Avel* 14:5). We should provide the patient with food that tastes good, and we should feed the patient on time (*Yakira D'chaya* 3:4). And when we pay our visit, we should discuss only cheerful topics (*Yakira D'chaya* 3:6). The Talmud also lists some types of illness that were considered so serious that a visit might be too difficult for the patient.

Jewish tradition teaches us that one of the most significant things we can do for a sick person is to offer a prayer at his or her bedside. In the second century, Rabbi Jose wrote the following because he thought that a prayer for all sick people was most likely to be answered: "May God have mercy upon you in the midst of the sick of Israel" (*Shabbat* 12b). When we take our children to visit a sick relative or friend, we can teach them to say Rabbi Jose's prayer. Our kids can also learn to say the traditional blessing: *Barukh atah Adonai Rofei Hakholim* (Blessed is the Lord, Source of Healing).Whether or not they are able to visit personally, they can ask a rabbi to say *Mi Sheberakh* (The One Who Blesses), a special prayer for a sick person, during the Torah service in synagogue.

We can begin to teach young children this mitzvah when a friend of theirs stays home from school because of illness. We can help our youngsters call their friend to cheer him or her up or we can encourage them to send a homemade card. Older children can offer to bring home books from school or to make copies of class notes. These gestures help our children demonstrate their caring and thoughtfulness.

Sometimes we hesitate to take our young children to visit someone who is quite ill. We worry about frightening or upsetting them. But children are often more resilient and aware than we give them credit for being. If everyone in our household is upset about a sick relative or friend, it can be better to let our children visit the patient than for the child to imagine something awful. A short visit, at a carefully chosen time, can sometimes allay our children's fears while giving them the opportunity to participate in this very meaningful mitzvah.

We should also encourage our children to try to reach out to the sick people in our community. Depending on our children's ages, they can send holiday cards to a nursing home or hospital; collect and donate toys, books, and stuffed animals to a children's hospital; or arrange a visit to read to or to play games with patients in a cancer unit. We can teach our children to ask about the sick or hospitalized members of our synagogue and then help them find a way to help out or to cheer up those patients.

Giving Tzedakah

Although tzedakah is often translated as "charity," this is not really correct. The word "charity" comes from the Latin *caritas,* meaning "love." But the word "tzedakah" comes from the Hebrew word *tzedek,* which means "righteousness" and "justice." We often are motivated to give charity out of feelings of caring for others. But we give tzedakah because it is the right and just thing to do.

The Torah commands us to "open your hand to the poor and needy kinsman in your land" (Deuteronomy 15:11). It is an injustice if we are able to give but don't. To engage fully in a deed of lovingkindness, we should act from our hearts. But even when we give without a heartfelt spirit, we are still being helpful. As we develop the habit of giving tzedakah, we will learn to enjoy giving.

Jewish tradition contains guidelines for how one should give. The Rabbis understood that, if possible, we should save a person from needing the gift in the first place. The Talmud says, "He who lends money is greater than he who gives charity; and he who throws money into a common purse [to form a partnership with a poor person] is greater than either" (*Shabbat* 63a). Judaism also teaches that all of us, not just the wealthy, have the obligation to help others who are in worse circumstances. The Talmud says, "Even a poor man who himself survives on charity should give charity" (*Gittin* 7b) and "If a man sees that his livelihood is barely sufficient for him he should still give charity from it" (*Gittin* 7a). This is because tzedakah is so important that even poor people should have the opportunity to perform this mitzvah.

In the *Mishneh Torah,* Maimonides outlined the most famous guidelines for giving tzedakah. He identified eight levels of giving, each more worthy of praise than the one before it. The first level of giving is when we give with resentment. The second is when we give cheerfully but give less than we should. Third is when we give directly to the poor after being asked to give. Fourth, we give directly to the poor without being asked. The fifth level is when we do not know the recipient, but the recipient knows us. Sixth is when we know the recipient, but the recipient does not know us. The seventh level of giving is when we and the recipient do not know each other. And the highest level of giving is when we help the recipient find a way to no longer need tzedakah.

The idea of giving in a way that doesn't embarrass the recipient is a key feature in tzedakah. Rabbi Yannai saw a man giving a poor man a coin in public. He said, "It would have been better for you not to have given it to him than to have given it and put him to shame" (*Hagigah* 5a). And Rabbi Elazar said that some one who performs tzedakah in secret is greater than Moses (*Bava Batra* 9b). When we give in this way, we demonstrate the essence of lovingkindness: we care enough about others to provide not only for their needs but also for their souls. Recognizing that we can help maintain a person's dignity and self-respect, even while we offer essential financial support, turns an ordinary good deed into hesed.

Unlike other religions, Judaism does not teach that poverty is noble or good. The Talmud says, "If all the suffering and pain in the world were gathered [on one side of a scale] and poverty was on the other side, poverty would outweigh them all" (Exodus *Rabbah* 31:14). Perhaps the Rabbis understood that when we are in truly desperate circumstances, unable to provide the basic necessities of life for ourselves or our loved ones, we are unable to think about anything else.

When we teach our children about this mitzvah, we should discuss Maimonides' levels of giving tzedakah, helping our kids identify a modern example of each. This will allow them to understand the concept and make it easier for them to find opportunities to give themselves. We model tzedakah for our children when we give to both Jewish and secular causes. Even young children can be encouraged to help decide where our family'sa tzedakah will go.

The Talmud also teaches that "emissaries on their way to do a mitzvah will never come to harm" (*Pesachim* 8b). Because of this, we give travelers money to donate when they reach their destination. We can encourage our children to be both donors and distributors of tzedakah. This might even change the way they think about traveling.

TEACHING LOVINGKINDNESS

When we teach our children to seek every opportunity to perform deeds of lovingkindness we affect the way they relate to the world. We should help them realize that the feeling of satisfaction that comes from doing the right thing can light up their lives. All our children can participate in such deeds and feel very good about themselves as they make the world a better, more loving place.

Talk
About It

Judaism teaches that when we perform acts of lovingkindness, we are following the example that God has set for us. Hesed, however, means more than merely performing specific acts. Hesed is where our hearts meet the highway; it has to do with our attitudes as well as our actions. We teach our children that when they do deeds of lovingkindness, they should not measure, count, or look for payback. They must simply give their best from their hearts. We can begin to teach our children about hesed by helping them reflect on a time when someone did something for them that they would not be able to repay. We can also talk about a time when they did something for someone else without thinking about what benefit it might bring them.

Welcoming Guests

Offering hospitality to guests is a lovely way to give of ourselves. We teach our children that although it is a commandment, we can find joy when we invite others into our home. We can remind our children that we welcome guests not by being fancy or lavish but by demonstrating our pleasure at being able to share what we have. We can start a discussion about this mitzvah by asking our kids questions like these:

- Do you enjoy having guests?
- How do you make things special for them?

The More Mud, the Better (a Hasidic Tale)

Once, Rabbi Israel of Riszhyn was traveling with a group of his students. When they came to a town, one of the students mentioned that there was a rich man in the town who offered hospitality only to great men but not to poor ones. However, the student thought that when the man saw the great rabbi, he would take them in.

They went to the home of the rich man and knocked on the door, but the man did not open it. Then, the rabbi went around to the side of the house and knocked on a window. When the rich man saw who it was, he rushed to let him in. But the rabbi said, "My students also wish to come in."

"But look at their shoes. They're covered with mud and they'll dirty the whole house," the rich man cried.

"Let me tell you a story," the rabbi responded. "Once there was a rich man who was very stingy. He never allowed poor people into his home. But once, when he was on a journey, he passed a poor family whose wagon had turned over in the mud. He took them into his carriage and brought them to their destination.

"When the rich man died, the angels began counting up his acts of stinginess, which were almost without measure. Then one angel told the others about the poor family the man had helped on the road. Another angel put mud from their shoes on the scale of justice and it outweighed all of the man's sins. Only then were the angels able to let the rich man into Paradise."

When the rich man heard this, he began to tremble. Then he said to the rabbi and his students, "Come in. All of you are welcome. The more mud, the better!"

- What did the rich man learn from the rabbi's story?
- What lesson can you take from this story to use when you have the opportunity to offer hospitality?

What Would You Do?

PRESCHOOL CHILDREN

Miriam is inviting Hallie, a friend from school, for a sleepover for the first time. She wants Hallie to have a good time. Miriam knows that Hallie lives in a big beautiful house and has every new toy. Her own house and toys are not as fancy.

• What can Miriam do?
• What do you think will happen?
• What might be a menschlich thing for Miriam to do?
• What would you do?

ELEMENTARY-SCHOOL CHILDREN

Just before Passover, Alex hears his friend Ronny say that his family isn't going to his grandparents' house for Passover this year. Alex's family always has a big family seder.

• What are some things that Alex can do?
• What might happen if he does each of these things?
• How does your Judaism help you decide what to do?
• What do you think you would do?

ADOLESCENTS

Don wants to invite a bunch of his friends over to hang out on Saturday night. Usually, they go to Jordan's house because his parents are really casual and don't mind the loud music and voices. Don wants his friends to be comfortable in his home, but he knows that his parents are stricter than Jordan's.

• What are Don's options?
• What are the consequences of each option?

• What does Judaism suggest we do?
• How would you handle this?

Feeding the Hungry

When we share food with those who can't afford it, we have an opportunity to offer emotional as well as physical sustenance. We teach our children that when they offer more than is required and when they offer the best of what they have, they demonstrate their ability to offer lovingkindness. We can help our children understand the importance of feeding the hungry when we ask questions like the following:

• How do you feel when you see a person on the street asking for a handout for food?
• Have you ever volunteered at a shelter or soup kitchen?
• How do you feel about it?

Let Them Eat Stones (a Hasidic Tale)

A rich man once came to a rabbi and asked for the rabbi's blessing.

"How do you eat each day," the rabbi asked.

"Very simply," the rich man answered. "I eat only dry bread with a little salt."

"Dry bread and salt," the rabbi said. "Why don't you treat yourself better, since you are so wealthy?" The rabbi continued to tell the man that he should eat better food.

After the man left, the rabbi's students asked him what difference it made if the rich man ate only dry bread. The rabbi explained that it makes a very great difference.

"If he is used to rich foods, then he will understand that a poor man must at least have a dry crust of bread with a little salt. But, if he is used to only dry bread and salt, he will imagine that the poor can be satisfied with stones."

☙

- What do you think about the rabbi's explanation?
- What responsibility do you have to help feed the hungry?
- What do you give to people who are poor and hungry?

What Would You Do?

PRESCHOOL CHILDREN

Ari's Sunday-school class is collecting food for the kosher food pantry run by a Jewish organization in their town.

- What can Ari do?
- What do you think will happen?
- What might be a menschlich thing for Ari to do?
- What would you do?

ELEMENTARY-SCHOOL CHILDREN

Brianna notices that after snack at Hebrew school there is usually a lot of cake and fruit left over.

- What are some things that Brianna can do?
- What might happen if she does each of these things?
- How does your Judaism help you decide what to do?
- What do you think you would do?

ADOLESCENTS

Darren has to do ten hours of community service each year for school. Around the corner from the shelter where he volunteers, Darren sees a man begging for food on the street.

- What are Darren's options?
- What are the consequences of each option?
- What does Judaism suggest we do?
- How would you handle this?

Visiting the Sick

Our tradition teaches that whenever we visit a person who is sick, we help that person recover. Because our children have all been sick at one time or another, it is easy to help them understand how much a caring visit can mean to someone who is ill. We teach them that it shows people that they are not forgotten, that they mean something to us. We can explain to our kids that although it can be scary and upsetting to visit people who are very sick, it is those people who most need our time and attention. If a visit is not appropriate, we can help our children find other ways of demonstrating their concern. The following types of questions help us begin a dialogue with our children:

- What do you like people to do for you when you are sick?
- How have you showed your concern for someone who is sick?

Abraham and the Angels (a Legend from the Torah)

Abraham's tent had openings on all sides so that he could easily see travelers coming from any direction and invite them into his home. It gave him great happiness to provide food, drink, and shelter to weary travelers.

Once, when Abraham was sick, no travelers came to his home for several days. Abraham was concerned and sent his servant Eliezer out to search for anyone who was passing by and needed a place to stay. Eliezer could find no one. Abraham was so distressed that, despite his illness, he rose from his bed and went out to look himself.

Seeing Abraham's concern, God told the angels Gabriel, Michael, and Raphael to disguise themselves as men and meet Abraham on the road. When Abraham saw what he thought were three travelers, he ran to greet them and invited them to come to his tent.

Abraham quickly became so concerned with providing food and drink for his guests that he forgot all about his own illness. His pain and suffering seemed to disappear. His concern for others had overcome his own illness.

∞

- What does this story about Abraham teach us about caring for others?
- Why is it so important to show lovingkindness when someone is sick?

What Would You Do?

PRESCHOOL CHILDREN

Tim, a boy in Michael's class, has been sick all week. Michael would like to do something to show Tim that his friends miss him.

- What can Michael do?
- What do you think will happen?
- What might be a menschlich thing for Michael to do?
- What would you do?

ELEMENTARY-SCHOOL CHILDREN

Cindy's grandmother is in a nursing home. She likes to see Cindy, but Cindy doesn't like the smells, sounds, and the other sick people.

- What are some things that Cindy can do?
- What might happen if she does each of these things?
- How does your Judaism help you decide what to do?
- What do you think you would do?

ADOLESCENTS

One of the guys on Joe's basketball team was diagnosed with leukemia. His treatments have made him lose his hair, and he is thin, tired, and weak. Joe's coach has suggested a visit, but a lot of the guys on the team say that it makes them feel weird.

- What are Joe's options?
- What are the consequences of each option?
- What does Judaism suggest we do?
- How would you handle this?

Giving Tzedakah

Giving tzedakah usually involves giving money to someone less fortunate. We must show our children that Judaism teaches that there are a variety of ways of helping others and that helping the needy find a way to help themselves is the best tzedakah of all. When we teach our children about tzedakah, we can discuss the following types of questions:

- Why do you think it is better to help others help themselves than simply to give money?
- What experiences have you had giving tzedakah?

Charity Saves from Death (a Talmudic Tale)

A fortune-teller told Rabbi Akiva that a snake would bite his daughter on her wedding day and that she would die. As the day of the wedding came closer, the rabbi became more and more worried. On the day before the wedding, his daughter took off a pin she was wearing and stuck it into a fence. She did not know it, but the pin pierced the eye of a poisonous snake that was hidden there. The next morning, when she pulled out the pin, the snake was stuck on it.

Akiva asked his daughter, "What good deed did you do to deserve such a reward?"

His daughter answered, "Yesterday a beggar came to our door. Everyone was too busy preparing for the wedding feast to take care of him. So, I gave him my own portion."

Then Rabbi Akiva looked at his daughter and smiled. "You have performed a great mitzvah," he told her.

- Why is it such an important mitzvah to help someone less fortunate than us?
- How does this help us to become better people?

What Would You Do?

PRESCHOOL CHILDREN

Before Shabbat everyone in Megan's family puts money in the family tzedakah box. Megan's parents give her some coins so that she can give tzedakah and have some money to put in her bank.

- What can Megan do?
- What do you think will happen?
- What is a menschlich thing for Megan to do?
- What would you do?

ELEMENTARY-SCHOOL CHILDREN

Before they went shopping for new spring clothes, Johanna's mother asked her to clean out her closet. Johanna found a bunch of things that she had outgrown or didn't like anymore. A lady who cleans her mom's office has a daughter about Johanna's age and another a few years younger.

- What are some things that Johanna can do?
- What might happen if she does each of these things?
- How does your Judaism help you decide what to do?
- What do you think you would do?

ADOLESCENTS

Jake's dad owns a restaurant and has several jobs available for the summer. Jake found out that his friend Arianna's father just lost his job, but she's embarrassed and doesn't want anyone to know. Jake knows that she needs money for college in the fall.

- What are Jake's options?
- What are the consequences of each option?
- What does Judaism suggest we do?
- How would you handle this?

Living with Lovingkindness

Judaism teaches us that we can never perform too many deeds of lovingkindness, that there can never be too much kindness in the world. We teach our children that hesed can change their lives and the lives of those they touch with their good deeds. We can help our children see that as they open their hearts, as well as their hands, they can begin to change the world. We should encourage our kids to be on the look-out for opportunities to show lovingkindness.

6

Teach Our Children Diligently

For the Lord grants wisdom;
knowledge and discernment are by God's decree.
—Proverbs 2:6

*H*okhmah, wisdom, is the virtue that unlocks all others. It
includes understanding the world and ourselves. It is insight
and perception, or "getting it", as our kids would say. It encompasses
book learning and street smarts and practical know-how and technical knowledge, but wisdom is more than any one or even all of these
combined. Wisdom is more than knowing how to do things; it is also
knowing what to do and when to do it. It is understanding how to live
with ourselves and how to live properly with others. Acquired in
many ways throughout our lives, wisdom is not the exclusive domain
of the old, the accomplished, or the scholarly.

Judaism greatly honors wisdom, counseling: "One should ask for
wisdom above all other virtues, for it contains everything else" (Song
of Songs *Rabbah* 1:1, 9). Solomon, shortly after he became king,
dreamed that God appeared to him and offered to give him whatever
he wanted. Solomon replied that, most of all, he desired "an understanding mind . . . to distinguish between good and bad" (1 Kings
3:5–14). Pleased with this response, God promised to give him riches
and honor as well as wisdom.

Our tradition teaches us that we should try to acquire wisdom in many different ways and from every possible source. Ben Zoma said, "Who is wise? One who learns from everyone" (*Pirke Avot* [*Ethics of Our Fathers*] 4:1). Judaism tells us that wisdom is found in many places and forms, that many different types of people have something of value to convey to us. We must not limit ourselves solely to traditional scholars and scholarship, although knowledge of that sort is part of wisdom.

Jews define ourselves as "the People of the Book." This book, the Torah, is the traditionally Jewish source of all wisdom. It contains our history, and a great part of wisdom is what we can learn from the past. The Torah also contains the laws that are meant to guide our ideals and values and teach us how to live. Yet we can know the Torah's words without truly comprehending its wisdom. The study of Torah and the pursuit of the wisdom it contains, is a means to acquire all of the other virtues. As Hillel said, "An ignoramus can't be righteous." As we learn the Torah, we must make it our blueprint for the future; when it informs our understanding of how to live a menschlich life, we have begun to acquire wisdom.

Wisdom also means understanding practical information about the world. Wise people may not be technical geniuses, but they understand how the world functions. They have acquired street smarts and have a trade or profession to support themselves in a way that satisfies their needs. They also are wise about people; they understand what makes others tick. Wise people are sensitive to human needs and motivations, fears and desires. They know when to speak and when to keep silent. And when they speak, they know what to say and how to say it. And the wise understand themselves; they have insight into their own hearts and minds. They know their strengths and weaknesses and are able to maximize the first and minimize the second.

In the Book of Job (28:28), we read: " 'See! Fear of the Lord is wisdom; to shun evil is understanding.'" Ultimately, wisdom comes from God and our human wisdom is limited. Eugene Borowitz, in *The*

Jewish Moral Virtues, wrote that the greatest wisdom is knowing when our own wisdom is insufficient and understanding that we can turn to God and sense what to do.

WHAT IS WISDOM AND
HOW DO WE ACQUIRE IT?

Wisdom is more than a collection of facts or an accumulation of skills. We have wisdom when we understand the larger picture of how the world works. We can be intelligent without being wise. Wisdom is the ability to comprehend, on a deep and profound level, the universe and all that it holds.

Judaism teaches that we recognize a wise person by his actions. "Wise people are recognized by their speech" (*Derekh Eretz Zuta* 5:3). They know the right thing to say and when and how to say it. And we learn that "it isn't necessary to tell a wise man to hold his tongue" (*Derekh Eretz Zuta* 7:4); there can be great wisdom in thoughtful and companionable silence. Sometimes there are no appropriate words, and wisdom is understanding which time is which.

The Talmud teaches us that a wise person is "one who can see what is coming" (*Tamid* 32a). When we are wise, we learn from our experiences and change our behaviors, attitudes, and beliefs. We understand that, "A dullard repeats his folly" (Proverbs 26:11) and we try to "Be not like the fool who, after sinning, brings an offering but does not repent" (*Berachot* 23a).

Judaism teaches us to "love the one who rebukes us, so that we may add to our wisdom" (*Derekh Eretz Zuta* 9:2). This is difficult, yet, if we are closed-minded and defensive, instead of open to constructive criticism and advice, we shut ourselves off from learning and acquiring wisdom. Ultimately, Judaism teaches us that the wiser we get, the wiser we get. "God gives the wise their wisdom and knowledge to those who know" (Daniel 2:21). We have the wisdom to recognize what we don't know and the wisdom to want to change. Acquiring wisdom is a lifelong journey, a process that never ends. And when we are truly wise, we know this and rejoice in the experience. "If a person imagines that he has attained it [wisdom], he is a fool" (Sh'lomo ibn Gabirol, *Mivhar Hapeninim*).

We can teach our children that there are three traditionally Jewish sources of wisdom: Torah, prayer, and work. *Pirke Avot* (5:22) tells us "Turn it [Torah] over and over again for one can find everything in it." Much more than a collection of stories and laws, the Torah contains insights into human nature and the wisdom of the ages. The Torah gives us all we need to know to live a fully Jewish and fully menschlich life. Our rabbis and scholars have studied, interpreted, and reinterpreted the Torah for thousands of years, and when we begin to study the Torah, we acquire wisdom and we realize that there is always more to learn and understand.

We can also acquire wisdom through *tefilah,* prayer. Prayer is not about God; it is about us. God, it has been said, does not need our prayers; we need them because they help us understand ourselves. As we open our hearts to God and the universe, prayer helps us focus on and appreciate our minds, bodies, and spirits, and the world in which we exist. We each have own approach to prayer: Some of us sit in silence, others sing or dance, and some recite the traditional words of our people in English or Hebrew. Whatever our style, it matters only that our prayer touches our deepest selves.

We also acquire wisdom about the world and our place in it through *malakhah,* work. Our jobs are more than simply a means of providing for our families. Through our work, we gain wisdom about ourselves and others. Our work helps us understand our own strengths and weaknesses through our tenacity, inventiveness, competitiveness, cooperativeness, poise, and maturity. And when we test ourselves through our work and find ourselves wanting, we use our wisdom to help us find the strength, inspiration, resources, and determination to continue on or to start over again.

We acquire a great deal of wisdom about other people by understanding our colleagues and competitors in the work world. We learn who is smart, honest, and hardworking and who is not. We discover who appreciates cooperation and teamwork and who does not. And we learn how to deal with each of these people and situations.

When we have a combination of Torah study, prayerful introspection, and satisfying work in our lives, the wisdom we acquire from each magnifies the wisdom we gain from the others.

HOW DO OUR CHILDREN LEARN ABOUT LEARNING?

As with each of the other virtues, we must model the acquisition of wisdom for our children. Judaism teaches us that wisdom comes in many forms and that we should learn from many different people and circumstances. We must demonstrate this in our daily interactions with our kids and others. Our children see us learning from books we read and by talking with friends and colleagues. They see us at prayer and practicing Jewish rituals. And from these experiences, they learn how to gain their own wisdom. We can help them feel the excitement of discovering for themselves some new piece of information or a successful solution to a problem. When they see us learn from people who have a wide variety of skills, achievements, and experiences, they realize that wisdom can be gained from all those we meet.

Our behavior is especially important in the case of Torah learning and prayer. If we want our children to take their Jewish education seriously, then they must see us attending services, observing the holidays, taking adult education classes, and reading Jewish stories. If instead, we drop our children off for Saturday morning services, while we do the grocery shopping, our kids learn that we do not value our Jewish rituals. Our children learn the importance we attach to acquiring Jewish wisdom by the way we live our own lives.

When we model our working lives for our children we must be careful that we keep our careers in perspective. Many of us are driven by material success; some of us work to prove ourselves to the world, and others use our work to define who we are. But we need to show our children that family and God are also important to us. One way to teach our children this lesson is to keep Shabbat. As we learn in Exodus (20:9–10), "Six days you shall labor and do all your work, but the seventh day is a sabbath of the Lord your God: you shall not do any work." We model this commandment by spending the day in prayer, Torah study, and/or contemplation of ourselves and the world, acquiring wisdom as we enjoy Shabbat.

While we keep our working lives in perspective, we must help our kids keep theirs in perspective, too. School is our kids' work, and although we want our children to do well in school, we should be careful about placing too much pressure on our children over their academic success. We should help our children see that their grade-point average is but one aspect of who they are and that it does not reflect how wise they are. We may be surprised to find that when our children can relax and enjoy school for learning's sake instead of for making a certain grade, they may begin to excel.

As parents, we often try to save our children from acquiring life's wisdom the hard way—by learning from their mistakes. However, this is sometimes the only way our children can gain certain wisdom. While we do need to make sure that our children are safe and will not harm others, we also need to allow them to make their own mistakes. In this way they will begin to recognize and trust their own strength, skill, and savvy.

WISDOM OR ACTION: WHICH IS BETTER?

"Rabbi Hannania ben Dosa used to say: 'Those who value right action over the pursuit of wisdom—their wisdom endures. Those who value the pursuit of wisdom over right action—their wisdom will not endure' (*Pirke Avot* 3:11), and " 'Those whose deeds exceed their wisdom, their wisdom is enduring, but those whose wisdom exceeds their deeds, their wisdom is not enduring' " (*Pirke Avot* 3:12). Judaism makes a critical and basic connection between wisdom and action, thoughts and deeds.

Wisdom acquired solely for its own sake, that doesn't produce any-

embedded into my forehead. I could feel my face swelling faster by the second. My entire body stung and pulsed as if it had been scrubbed with sandpaper. I looked at the tweezers as he pulled them away—he was picking out bits of broken glass.

More cops showed up. A black guy got out of his car and walked up to Tristan. He said hello, then leaned close to my face and laughed. He had a gap in his front teeth and smelled of cigarettes. Tristan gave him an impatient look. The black officer shrugged, then walked back to the rest of the cops.

"Your boss gave us a call," Tristan said. "I was only expecting to see a shouting match."

I smiled and thought: only now did Steve have a reason to call the police on you.

Conrad was handcuffed and put in another car. They had taken his shirt off to look at the wound I had made. My bite looked like a purplish-red football on his back. The extra cops stood around and talked to each other.

"Am I being arrested?" I asked.

Tristan nodded. "Sorry." He dabbed my face with cotton balls dipped in witch hazel. Then he dragged a scratchy, dry towel down my face a couple times. "Once this bleeding stops, you'll be OK." He wiped my face again then stuck a few Band-Aids to my forehead. "You can go to the hospital, if you want."

"I'm fine," I said, but I wasn't. If I'd said I was hurt, it might have led to more questions that I didn't think I had the energy to answer.

Tristan asked me to stand and put my hands on the trunk of his car. He read me my rights and bound my hands together with a white plastic drawstring—handcuffs wouldn't have fit over my cast.

The car Conrad was in drove off. I watched his head bob up and down in the back seat as the car splashed through rain-filled potholes.

Tristan sat me in the back of his squad car; there were no door handles. The spinning lights on the roof sounded like two large marbles rumbling against each other. The CB next to his steering wheel beeped and fizzed with static. Tristan got in the front seat and cleared his throat before starting the engine.

I looked back at RHP. The tele-operators were all watching from the windows. Steve stood outside on the dock among the shippers, his arms folded. He shook his head and slumped his shoulders. I thought he was upset that he had to call the cops on us.

The first of the afternoon trucks pulled into the parking lot. The driver was the man that had thrown a soggy banana at me. He looked like he was in a hurry—as if he had once again promised his wife that he'd pick up their kid from school. I remembered the pile of boxes in the middle of the shipping area; it still hadn't been broken down for the trucks. Now I understood why Steve looked upset.

I WAS TAKEN around the back of the station to a small office. The floors were streaked with black marks from rubber-soled combat boots. A dripping air conditioner rattled above the steel door. Tristan handcuffed my good wrist to a lead pipe that was cemented to the wall next to his desk. I sat on a wooden chair that had warped veneer on the backrest; it crackled when I sat back. There was a row of lockers behind the desk, on top of which were black cans of mace. One officer had his dry-cleaned uniform covered in plastic hanging on one of the locker doors. Behind me was a little room where they took mug shots. And in front of me and to the right was a cage door that led to the cells.

Tristan was filling out a piece of paper that had PRISONER'S ARREST RECORD printed across the top. It had spaces for my height, weight, complexion, eye color, and any scars or tattoos I may have had. I thought of what the Indian doctor at the hospital had told me about having a prominent scar on the back of my hand—I wondered if I should have mentioned it. For my address and name and date of birth, Tristan used my license that he had taken back at RHP. I noticed on the bottom of the paper there was a place for behavior; it had three boxes: cooperative, uncooperative, and agitated. I was checked off as being a cooperative prisoner. I felt oddly proud of myself.

Tristan set his pen on the desk and stood. He undid my cuffs, then had me empty everything out of my pockets. I set a couple of dollar bills and my car keys on the desk, and he listed them on the back of the arrest record. Then he put everything into a plastic sandwich bag.

"Let's get you printed and your picture taken." Tristan led me to the small photo room. There was a veneered counter to the left with silver trim around the edges. A pad of black ink for fingerprinting prisoners was recessed into the top. There was an empty gun cage on the wall and a sign that had a cartoon drawing of a camera with arms and legs and a huge smile—it said something about juveniles not having to be photographed.

It was hard for both of us to move around in the room, especially because Tristan had to keep hold of my arm. The full yellow light above us flickered and buzzed.

Tristan set a white card with green lettering on the table. He started with my right hand, rolling each finger in the ink then doing the same on the space on the card. It hurt the way he had to twist my wrist to get the print to go on evenly.

"Can I do the left hand?" I asked. "It still hurts."

He nodded. "Just roll your fingers—don't smudge it."

I did each finger, and Tristan watched me closely, holding his tongue between his front teeth, hoping I wouldn't mess up.

I had to put four fingers on each hand simultaneously at the bottom of the card. My fingers were greasy from the ink. I looked around the cramped room and noticed that black finger smudges were everywhere—on the walls, on the tin paper towel dispenser, there were even a few hand-prints on the ceiling.

There wasn't a sink in the room, so I had to wash my hands with some liquid soap that was mounted under the desk. It was a gallon tub that had a drawing of an orange slice on the label and smelled like orange taffy. Tristan helped me get the ink off my hands, because I couldn't really knead my hands together to work up a lather. I wiped the soap off with a brown paper towel. My hands were stained gray-orange.

For my picture, I stood behind a sign that was attached to a pole that slid up and down, to adjust to your height. The sign had black dials with white numbers. Tristan rolled the dials so it matched the number on my arrest card: 27513, with the date written under that in marker on a piece of notebook paper.

He took one picture of me facing front, then two profile shots. The exposed pictures came out of the back of the camera. He slid back a latch and a black piece of paper came out. He sat all three pictures on the desk and let them develop.

"You get a phone call now," he said. "You can use the one on my desk, just make sure you call collect even if it's local."

"There's nobody to call," I said, testing the stickiness of the orange soap on my hands by pinching my fingers together.

"You got no relatives to call, no friends?"

"I do," I said. "But I don't want them to see me here."

He shrugged, letting it show on his face that he thought it was a bad decision, and walked me out of the photo room. Then Tristan told me I had a choice of either taking off my shoes while I was in my cell or I could just take out my laces. "I'd just take off my laces," he said in a hush. "Some guys defecate on the floors—and we don't bother cleaning it too well."

He led me through the cage door to the first cell on the right. I had to shuffle my feet as I walked or my boots would have fallen off. Tristan carried a single fat key on a large metal loop. All the cells were to the right. The wall facing the cells was made of glazed brick, with a mint-green rotary phone on a mismatched beige cord mounted all the way at the ceiling. Tristan swung open the heavy door, which moaned on its hinges. He held a hand out, and I stepped inside.

I turned around and watched the iron door seal shut with a soft thud. "What happens to me now?"

"You can either make bail, which is five hundred dollars, or the commissioner will decide what to do with you."

"When's he come in?"

"Could be hours; could be days." He tapped on the bars and raised an eyebrow. "Let me know if you need a phone call." He turned the key in the lock, then tugged the door a couple of times to make sure it was secure. His round glasses slipped down and he pushed them back up with one finger. "I'll be at my desk," he said and walked off. The cage door clanged shut behind him.

The bunks in my cell were two concrete slabs fitted to the beige cinder-block walls. I stood there and wiggled my toes in my loose boots. There were no lights in the cell. People had scratched initials and obscenities into the paint on the walls with their fingernails. An aluminum toilet with a tiny sink attached sat so close to the bottom bunk that you had to step over it to reach the wall. The urine in the toilet was the color of cider. The smell got into my hair and snaked into my pores. There was a button to flush it on the wall under a bolted-shut fuse box. I pressed the button, and the toilet made a low gurgling sound, then the piss bubbled, like someone blowing a straw into chocolate milk. Then it settled again. I sat as far away from the toilet as possible, with my face turned to the painted-black iron bars, smelling the coffee from the office.

I could tell there were other prisoners in the cells that went down the hallway, but nobody talked. A few times I heard feet swishing on the concrete floors and a few throat-clearing coughs, to break up the silence. I wondered if my neighbor was here.

I rested my back against the wall. I wanted to sleep, but I was in too much pain. My mouth felt wrecked. I rubbed my tongue along my teeth and gums, to feel the damage. My bottom front teeth were loose; I could wiggle them back and forth with my tongue, as if they were only hanging on by threads of nerves. The insides of my cheeks had stopped bleeding on the drive over, but I could still taste the steely blood in my saliva. Where my teeth cut into the insides of my mouth every time Conrad punched me, ragged meaty chunks of skin dangled. I picked them off with my fingers, tasting the oily ink and bitter soap. The bleeding started again. I stood up and spat into the steel sink, a glob of white bubbles streaked with red. I found it hard to spit without having a line of drool run down my chin. Then I noticed there was a tooth stuck in the drain. It had been broken in half, yellow on the outside, white along the break. The roots were stained with a layer of gums.

I sat back near the door and told myself to just spit on the floor from now on. My face was so swollen it hurt to open my mouth. I sat there and felt my cheeks balloon up. Coming into the barracks, Tristan had given me a wet paper towel that had been frozen. I had held it to my face until it melted and he took it away.

The thick smell of urine had started to get to me. It fused with the candy-orange smell of my hands into an indescribably bad odor. I stuck my face as far as I could through the bars, like a kid trying to get his head through the banisters in his house. The bars cast bands of shadows onto my arms. I looked straight ahead to the glazed tan wall of the hallway, and tried to forget where I was.

After a few minutes, I heard a voice in the cell next to me.

"Who's over there?" he whispered.

I didn't answer. I knew it was Conrad.

"Tom?" he asked. "Are you there? I got to talk to you." He waited for me to say something. When I didn't, he let the air out of his lungs in a sigh. "Can I please explain? I did everything I did for a reason. Just let me tell you."

"No," I said.

"*Please*," he cried. "My wife was going to leave me." I didn't respond, but he kept talking, anyway. "She called me about a month ago and told me that she wouldn't be there after I got released from the house." He paused, waiting for me to say something. "Do you hear me?" he hissed. "My goddamn wife was leaving me!"

"Good," I said. "About time she came around."

"I know you don't mean that."

"I don't?"

"You have a right to be pissed. But . . ." He began to say something else, but he stopped himself.

I listened to him start and restart a bunch of sentences, looking for the right way to say what he had to say. I just stared at the shadows on my arms.

"I had to prove to her that I was making changes," he said finally. "I had to show her that I wasn't going to be a shipper for the rest of my life. The night she said she was leaving me, I lied and told her I had been promoted. I didn't know what else to do." He was crying already. I wanted him to just shut up so I could get some sleep. "She seemed so happy that I couldn't tell her the truth. Goddamnit, I can't lose my *kids*!" He blubbered for a bit, sucking in air in sharp gasps. He was crying so hard it sounded like he was laughing. "I turned you in so I could get your job." Someone down the hall told him to shut up.

"How did you know I was paid extra on that check? Terry said all that stuff is kept in Glen Burnie."

He sniffed. It sounded like mud being sucked through a tube. "I hired my roommate."

"The Pentagon guy?"

Conrad made a dog-like whimpering noise as a way of saying yes. "As long as I signed him in and out on the house's log, so he could stay out as late as he wanted, he agreed to help."

"How did he get my records?"

"I don't know," he blubbered. "He just made a phone call."

I remembered what his roommate had said to me when I called from Ocean City, about my problems only being a phone call away from being solved. I now knew what he meant—he was offering his help to stop Conrad.

"He got me your file, your time sheets, and a list of the amounts of all your paychecks."

Thinking of the furtive ex-Pentagon guy stealing my information made my palms sweat. I felt queasy knowing that a man who had taught people how to fake their deaths had access to my financial information. I could picture him meeting some old colleague in a restaurant and slipping manila folders to each other under a table.

"I searched through the pages all night," Conrad went on. "And I found that Thanksgiving you were paid but didn't work. Then I showed it to Steve, and he started the paper trail on you."

"How long ago did you show him?"

"About a week before we were hiding up on the roof. I wanted you to go down to talk to him about the shippers doing the clean-up, hoping you'd piss him off enough that he'd bring it up. But you didn't go down, so you kind of pissed away my plans. So I talked to him again on Monday morning."

"Didn't Steve want to know where you got these checks?"

"I tried to make it sound like I was fed up with you. I told Steve that when you got paid for the Thanksgiving you didn't work, you waved the check in our faces, bragging that you ripped off the company." He sniffed again, but he was all cried out. "I said that I stole the check from you and copied it. Did my best to make it seem like I was looking out for the company."

"So did I even have to pay the money back?"

"No," he said. "They took the eighty dollars on the chin."

"But you said it was over two hundred."

Conrad laughed sheepishly. "That was how much Terry's doctor bill was. Originally, I just wanted to get you fired, and you wouldn't have to pay a dime. But Terry was going to sue me for putting the trap on his seat. So I came up with the extra money at the last minute, to pay his doctor's bill."

My mouth hung open. I thought of that fold of skin on his back that I had bitten, and wished that I had ripped it off. Any chance of me forgiving Conrad blew away like sand. Everything that was wrong with his life he brought on himself. He put Terry in the hospital for a laugh; he wanted my job, so he got me fired. And when he got caught by Terry's family, he thought nothing of ripping me off to pay the doctor.

"I needed the goddamn money—I'm sorry. What did you want me to do?"

I laughed at him.

"And I'm sorry I had to rough you up. You shouldn't have came after me like that."

"You were hitting me like you hated me."

"I don't *hate* you," he said. "I just got caught up with everything—my wife, the house, bills. I didn't see you anymore. All I saw was every shitty thing about my life that's all gone wrong, rolled into one person. I took it out on you, and I'm sorry." Conrad sounded so insincere I could picture him rolling his eyes as he said this. "It was just a fight. Don't take it so personally."

"So," I said, not wanting to talk about the fight anymore, because it was most personal thing I had ever experienced, "after all this, did your wife even take you back?"

Conrad paused. "No. She left for Ohio two days ago. Took the kids with her."

I laughed.

Conrad shook his cell door, a soft rattling sound. "Don't

laugh, asshole!"

I couldn't help it. I opened my mouth and exploded, feeling the swollen skin of my face stretch, and the cuts in my mouth bleed again.

Conrad kicked the bars. "Don't *laugh*!" he barked, and the guy down at the end of the hallway told him to shut up again.

"You lost your wife and kids, and you're still stuck at RHP," I said. "Enough to drive a man to drink."

"You can shut your goddamn mouth!"

"You'll be needing those Polaroids of your wife, Connie. That's all that's left." I rested my forehead on the cold steel bars and let my laughing splutter out. "Knowing that she dumped your stupid ass makes this whole mess worth while."

I wasn't sure if I was truly mad at Conrad, or just thought I was supposed to be. But I knew I had to let him know that our friendship had dissolved right there in our separate cells. I did this by telling him that he should kill himself. I told him he should just be a drunk, because it's the only thing that he could do well. I told him any mean-spirited thing I could that I knew would hurt any chances of us ever forgiving each other. And I didn't mean a thing I was saying. The words seemed to float just beyond the bars, close enough for me to see their ugliness, but far enough out of my reach that I couldn't take them back.

Conrad never said another word to me. He just let me go on and on. The person at the end of the hall now told me to shut up. But I just kept on. I felt like a madman setting fire to a photo album—plastic pages turning with the heat, flashing pictures of Conrad on the dock and in my apartment. Images of Conrad twisted in the air like glowing embers outlined in sparks and fire. With every mean thing I said, the fire seemed to spread, making things between us beyond repair. As his image bubbled over in brown and black spots, his face faded from my memory, along with my anger. All that was left was exhaustion.

I WOKE TO THE SOUND OF THE CAGE DOOR in the hallway whining on its hinges. Shoes clicked on the ground, then came to a halt. I looked to my wrist to see what time it was, but I didn't wear a watch now that I had a cast over my arm.

The silhouette of a man stood in front of my cell. He put a key in the door and popped the lock. The door swung open, and he stood to one side.

"Time to go," he said, voice deep and coarse. I could smell cigarette smoke on him.

I could only see through bruised, swollen slits. Everything was dark and blurry. My whole face had gone stiff and sore while I had slept. I went to speak and winced under the pain in my mouth. "Are you the commissioner?" My loose front teeth clicked together when I closed my mouth, and my eyes jammed shut from the pain.

The man tapped his foot. "Someone posted your bond," he said.

I wanted to ask who, but it hurt too much to talk. I stood up and took a step forward, and my foot slipped out of my boot.

The man breathed out impatiently. I saw that it was the black cop that had laughed in my face when Tristan was bandaging me. When I stepped into the light, he bugged his eyes and laughed at me again. His face was still a blur. I felt like a mole stepping out into the sun.

He took me into the office and set the plastic bag with my keys, wallet, and money on the desk. I had to sign and date the back of the arrest record, stating that I had received all my property. I squinted around the room with my puffy eyes. Three teenagers sat on a bench by the door, handcuffed and shackled. When I squinted at them, one boy mumbled, "Jesus," under his breath.

I wanted a mirror to see how bad my face looked, but I doubted this cop would give me one. I wondered if Tristan was still here. I saw a flash go off in the mug shot room. Then I heard him tell someone to face right and to stop laughing.

The cop checked the box marked BOND on the HOW RELEASED part of the arrest record. His pen made sharp scratching sound on the paper.

"What happened to the guy who was in the cell next to me?" I asked, face throbbing as my lips made out the words.

The cop didn't answer. He was writing on the card with my

fingerprints on it.

"Did someone bail him out?"

The cop still didn't answer. He set a stainless steel clipboard with a yellow piece of paper on it. "Sign this," he said making an X at the bottom of the page. I signed it, and he gave me the pink copy.

"Well, is he still here?" I asked.

The cop sighed and started shuffling papers. "Clocked out ten minutes ago. This is *my* time. You can leave now."

"Can you even tell me who bailed me out?"

He glared at the top of his desk. "If you would *read* the form I gave you."

I folded the paper and put in my back pocket, then walked to the door before he said another word. When I got to the door, I groped for the knob like a blind man, bracing myself for the bright sun. But when I stepped outside, the sky was black. Sensor lights glowed yellow in the humidity of the parking lot like giant dandelions. The windows of the office buildings around me were dark. Everything appeared as if I were looking through a film of wax. The headlights of the cars on the street spread pearl-colored washes on the pavement.

I took the pink form out of my pocket and tried to read it. Tristan hadn't charged me for fighting or assault. Instead, he gave me a two-hundred-dollar citation for trespassing on the property of the shipping yard next to RHP. The ticket said I could go to court in Towson or just pay the fine. I scanned the paper for the name of the person who had posted my bail. In a box for release information, there were two spaces—one for a last name and one for the first name. In the first space, the name GREENE was written. I got excited, thinking it might have been Fritz. Then I read the name in the next blank, and I rubbed my eyes, thinking I was reading it wrong. The first name of the person who had bailed me out was SANDY. The tattoo of the girl on Fritz's arm flashed in my mind.

I squinted at the parking lot. Cars and pavement were muddled. I couldn't see where the tops of the building ended and the sky began. How would she even know who I am? I wondered. What does she want with *me*?

I heard a car door creak open then shut. I tried to focus my eyes, but everything was blurry-edged, as in a dream. I saw a little white truck parked under a steel street light. It was a rusty Datsun, just like the one Greg had driven to Joe's.

Leah walked over and stopped about ten feet away from me. Her glance went from my face to my dirty cast to my face again. "What have you been *doing* to yourself?" She stepped forward and touched my cheek. "Your *face*." She hugged me.

I didn't hug back. My arms hung at my sides.

Leah let me go. She looked down at the smudges of dirt on her shirt, rubbed off from my filthy clothes. She had on a white tank top with green trim around the neck and a pair of jeans. Her feet were bare. She brushed the dirt off her shirt then wiped her hands on the front of her pants. Wind scattered her hair in her face.

"I don't know what's going on," I said.

Leah rubbed her goose-bumped arms and looked at her feet. "I told my dad everything," she said, nodding to the ground. "I told him I was staying at my grandmother's; told him about the baby. I even told him I tried to have an abortion."

"Was he mad?"

She shook her head. "He was mad that I didn't tell him. But he said there was no point in being angry with me for getting pregnant." She looked back up; her eyes were bloodshot and tired. "I moved back home. Mom and Dad will help me raise the baby."

"What about Ron?"

Leah smiled without showing any teeth, but her eyes remained sad. I could tell that he was gone.

I went to say I was sorry, but she cut me off.

"I really *tried* to have an abortion," she said. "I'm not doing this for attention or because I'm stupid. I've been in the waiting room a dozen times, trying to move out of the chair when the doctor was ready. I even got undressed one time and let a nurse examine me. But I could never do it." She looked up at the sky and stretched her neck. "That night you found me on the bus—I had been in the parking lot of an abortion clinic all day. I sat on the curb and prayed for the guts to just go through with it."

We stayed quiet for a long time. Leah didn't look as if she was going to cry, but I could tell talking about this was wearing on her.

"How did you find me?"

"My dad took me to Joe's. I figured we still had things to talk about."

"No, how did you find me *here*?" I asked, pointing to the space on the ground between us.

"Joe said he'd lend me a truck." She frowned, suddenly distracted. "He's strange, isn't he?"

I nodded.

"He said that if I didn't come back with you and all your things, I had to pay him fifty dollars for gas and wear on the truck."

A smile muscled its way onto my puffy face.

"He seems to like you," she said. "He told me he misses you."

"No, he didn't," I said.

"Well, no. Not exactly. But I could tell."

I looked up at the dark sky and couldn't get rid of my smile. "He still wants me?"

Leah nodded and stepped forward. I could smell the cleanness of her hair. She was standing only a couple of inches away from me, so close I could feel the warmth of her body. "We all miss you," she said. "Uncle Fritz has been going nuts looking for you. He's the one who gave me directions to that RHP place. He said I might be able to get your address or phone number off somebody. But when I got there, some lady told me you were arrested for fighting. I called my uncle when I learned how much bail was, and he wired the money to a grocery store for me. He told me on the phone that if I couldn't get you to come back, he was going to come for you."

I held up the pink release form. "It says that Sandy Greene bailed me out."

"Yeah, that's me. But I've always gone by my middle name: Leah."

Leah backed away. "I wish it didn't have to be like this, but

I'm sorry. I know this isn't your problem. Still, I think . . ." Her voice trailed off into a murmur. It was as if she had been practicing what she wanted to say to me the whole ride up from Dewey, but now that the words left her mouth, it didn't feel right.

I stepped forward and rested my broken hand on her shoulder. She faced the ground, and tucked a few stray stands of hair behind her ear. Leah stepped forward and buried her face in my dirty, sweat-damp shirt. Her breath burned through the fabric. I put my chin on the top of her head. Her hair was soft and tickled my face in the wind. "Can you drive us somewhere?" I asked.

She nodded, breathing in my sweat and the dried dust from the puddle.

The salty air sealed my eyes shut. "My mom wants to meet you."

seventeen

FRITZ carried a four foot section of wall to the window. The edges of the two-by-fours jutting between the two slabs of sheet rock were ragged and blond. Fritz staggered as he pitched the awkward wreckage out. I listened as it crashed onto the grass, then started the reciprocating saw again. The blade gnashed through the studs and sheet rock. My eyeglasses fogged, and a yellow spray of sawdust prickled my lips. When the screaming motor whined down, Fritz took the piece of wall and heaved it out the window. It made me nervous when he did this, because he never looked outside to see if anybody was standing below. I set the saw on the plywood floor, and Joe came up behind me and looked at the open space where the wall had been.

The air was thick with dust and heat. Chips of wood and spare nails lay on the ground like confetti. My hands were cramped from using the saw, and the vibration of the motor still rattled through my bones, like an echo. Fritz wiped the sweat off his brow with the back of his forearm and rested, hands on hips, before going back to work.

It was now late August, and the apartment on the third floor of Joe's house was halfway complete. We had just knocked out a wall to make two of the smaller rooms into one big living room. All the stowed-away junk Joe had kept in here was now piled in the hallway, but the old smell of polish and mouse crap lingered. The room I had been sleeping in was to remain the same, although Leah and Mrs. Hartly were now giving it a coat of antique-white paint.

Joe walked over to where the wall we had just removed connected to the perpendicular wall. He rubbed his hand down the rough and ugly six inch gap. "Got to fill this with some drywall," he said, his voice bouncing in the empty room.

I heard an airplane's engine outside, cutting through the sky a mile above us. It drifted past over the trees, and we all kept still as its drilling motor was replaced with quiet. Only then did I feel exhausted. I rubbed the grit and sweat that had collected on my neck and wiped my hand on the back of my pant leg. It was three in the afternoon, and the sun had baked the house like pottery in a kiln.

We had opened all the windows, but every breeze that came in was miserable, like hot breath in our faces. Joe didn't have any air conditioning—didn't believe in it. He said he only liked the cool breeze of a window fan. If we wanted artificial cold, he had said, we could go bait trotlines.

I looked at Fritz, sweating and red-faced in his long-sleeved western shirt, and I wanted to throw him into the walk-in freezer, just to see if he'd bleed steam like an overheated engine. Fritz's hair hung in his face in sweaty blades. All day, as he cut drywall across the hall in what was to become my kitchen, his hair would flop in his face, he'd push it back, then it would fall again.

Although Fritz had cut all the drywall, I had to tack it to the walls. Joe didn't care that my wrist was still in a brace. He said that I was showing a lot of promise, but my hanging of drywall was shoddy at best.

"This way," he'd said, arms folded, "when you mess up, you're the only person who has to see it. It'll be a good incentive for you to get your act together."

Joe had been hard on me all summer. After returning from trotlining, he would give me lessons in the barn, teaching me how to cut dovetails for drawers with a router, how to make tenon shoulder joints with a table saw, and how to measure for pitch and run and rise. When I wasn't being taught how to use power tools, he had me read a volume of *Audel's Carpenters and Builders Guide* every week. On the boat, as I scooped crabs from the trotline, he'd quiz me.

"Black walnut, Tom?" he'd call out over the burping Volvo motor.

I'd say, "Used for interior finish and cabinet work."

Then Joe would change the questioning. "I was thinking of making a cofferdam to build another pier. . ."

"You'd want to use red spruce." Then when we'd get back, he'd make me build a cofferdam—or a stool or a bench or hip joints for rafters.

I didn't mind the work. It was interesting, and everyday I felt myself becoming more useful. In July, Joe even trusted me enough to go alone to a woman's house in Groves Burton, to build shelving in her walk-in closet. The woman's husband watched me the whole time and asked me questions about the tools I was using. He was friendly but unnerving. When he didn't have a question, he'd shake his head and say, "Bet I could do this if I had them fancy tools," just to break the silence. He even said this when I was using a hammer.

Joe stretched his back and yawned. "That's all for today."

At the mention of quitting, Fritz collapsed, arms flopping to his sides as if he were some machine that had just been un-plugged.

I went to the bedroom to check on Leah. From the hallway, I could hear Mike and Doug in the bathroom, giggling as they told each other jokes. They were replacing the pipes under the sink with PVC and copper.

"What do you name a girl with one leg shorter than the other?" Mike said.

"What?" Doug asked, already laughing.

"Eileen!" Mike burst forth, and on they jabbered like the blackbirds outside in the oak tree.

I opened the bedroom door. The smell of latex paint was sour and dizzying. Leah and Shelly (who wouldn't speak to me unless I called her by her first name) were sitting on the bed eating purplish stalks of rhubarb. There was a little saucer set between them with an ant hill-sized mound of sugar on it. Leah and I had furnished this room with some of the things Joe had in storage. I'd thrown almost all of my furniture from Baltimore away—everything except the clunky phone that had once caught fire. I now kept it on a dinner plate on a gum wood night table next to the bed. The plate was to protect the surface of the table in case the phone ever caught fire again.

Leah held up her arms. Her fingertips were dabbed white. "Like it?"

I looked around the room. The walls were glistening wet with paint. All the furniture had been scooted to the middle of the room. Joe had lent us a cheval dresser, a golden oak bed, and a washstand with a bevel-edged mirror. Joe said Leah and I could use these things for as long as we lived with him.

The only piece of furniture that Joe hadn't loaned us was a bookcase, which I had made out of some cull stock of Norway pine. When I had finished building it and staining it, I rubbed it with steel wool, then stained it again. Joe came into the barn after I had put on the second coat and said, "You better not be finished." He folded his arms and nodded at me. "You're a professional now. Professionals use no less than three coats of varnish."

This was the best compliment Joe had given me, because it didn't involve me showing promise or improving or progressing.

The bookcase looked empty, though. A few of my borrowed builder's guides were piled on the bottom shelf, and Leah kept a plant on it that was already dying. There were only two books on it that I owned. On the top shelf, I kept a copy of Bradford Waltz's memoir and a copy of *They Are Still Among Us*. I had bought the memoir off of Joe for two dollars. But I had found George Regal's book in a junk store in Groves Burton. A man had a table set up outside his shop, piled with milk crates filled with Billy Fury and Herman's Hermits records, the damp smell of basements and silverfish sunk deep into the sleeves. He had a velvet-lined suitcase filled with individually wrapped Doc Savage adventure novels, priced at ten to fifteen dollars a piece. Next to that was a grapefruit box with books that cost a nickel. I weeded through the junk on this table while I was waiting for Leah to get off work from Lewis's; she was a crab steamer and usually came home watery-eyed and smelling peppery. At the bottom of the grapefruit box, I found Dr. Regal's book. The pages were tan-brown at the edges, and the binding glue had dried up. But George Regal's superior half-smile was still clear on the front cover.

I didn't buy the book to read it. I just liked having it around. The sight of the aged and crumple-edged paperback sent me back to the spot on the floor next to my father's La-Z-boy. Sometimes, I'd pick it up and fan the pages across my face, just to breathe in its age and mustiness.

Fritz came in the room and sat on the floor in front of Shelly. She wrapped an arm around his neck and stuck a stick of rhubarb in his mouth.

Leah was wearing a paint-blotted bandanna over her hair. She held up a bitter stalk of rhubarb by the white end, but I shook my head. "Shouldn't you get started on dinner?" she asked. Fritz and Shelly looked over and agreed. Then they added that Leah should go help me.

I plopped down on the bed between Leah and Shelly. "I'll go in a minute."

"What are we having, anyway?" Fritz said.

There was a ham thawing on the chopping block in the kitchen, but before I could answer, Doug burst into the room. "They're here!" he said. "A truck just pulled onto the driveway." Mike came up behind him with his hands in a white towel.

Leah and I ran downstairs, and Mike and Doug followed behind us. Shelly and Fritz stayed put. As I was halfway down the stairs, I heard my door shut.

I stepped onto the porch and watched my brother's Dodge pick-up come to a stop on the dusty driveway. The ladders and tools in the bed shifted and clanged.

Strawberries were in bloom and lay in green bands in the fields. Leah stepped next to me and put a hand on the small of my back. Mike and Doug stayed further back on the porch, where there was shade.

The doors on my brother's truck had SHAWN BANNER—PRIVATE CONTRACTING in three-inch white vinyl letters. His windows were tinted as dark as mirrors. Leah walked down the steps, took off her bandanna, and stuffed it into the back pocket of her jeans. Then she combed her hair with her fingers and straightened her shirt.

My mother stepped out and staggered a bit until her cramped legs could support her weight. She tilted her head back to take in all of Joe's house, then had to put a hand on the hood to keep from falling back. Her hair was pulled back into a ponytail, streaked with a ribbon of gray. My mom put on a straw hat and shut the door. Leah ran over and gave her a kiss, but I stayed on the porch and waited for Shawn to step out.

After dinner, I wanted to take him out on the boat for some late night fishing. By this time I was catching catfish and blue snappers; toadfish didn't bother with me anymore. All day I'd hummed with nervous energy, waiting to take my brother on the boat to show off what I had learned. I daydreamed that Shawn would be clumsy with his fishing gear, then quiet with embarrassment after I'd shown him how to fix his lines. I imagined taking him into the barn while I made up the brine solution for the week. I'd even give him the honor of dropping the egg in the salty mix to see if it would stay afloat.

The driver side door opened. I hopped off the porch, no longer able to act calm, and Lisa stepped out of the truck. She shut the door, lips pressed tightly together, and tried not to look me in the eye. I walked over to her, unable to keep the disappointment from showing on my face. I dragged my feet through the gravelly pavement as I approached her.

Lisa shook her head before I could say anything. "He has a lot of work to do this weekend," she said soberly.

I pointed to the ladders and toolboxes in the pick-up. "But you've got his truck!"

"I'm sorry," she said, with a twinge of sadness and disgust drawing out the words. She stepped forward and grabbed my brace. "This about to come off?"

"In a week." I wanted to call Shawn's house just to catch him at home, with his television buzzing in the background.

Lisa scratched me softly under my chin. "Have we ever needed your brother to have fun?" she asked.

I nodded, then walked around the back of the truck to take

their bags.

JUST AS LEAH AND I were ready to go downstairs to eat that evening, I found Doug in my bathroom looking for cologne.

"I don't wear any," I told him.

"Well, do you have anything that smells nice?" he asked, briefly considering a can of shaving cream he had in his hand.

"What do you want to smell nice for?" I took the can from him and placed it back in the medicine cabinet.

"I just want to smell good." He toed an elbow joint of PVC on the floor that he'd install tomorrow. "*You're* wearing a dress shirt," he said. "Why do *you* have to look nice?"

"Because I'm having dinner with my mother."

"Well, if everybody downstairs is going to look nice, I don't want to stand out."

"Just tuck your shirt in and chew with your mouth closed," I said, but Doug didn't move. To look at him you'd think he was being asked to go downstairs without any pants. Really, he wanted the cologne to impress Lisa.

All day Doug had stumbled behind her as if he were being dragged by a foot of invisible wire. When I had driven Lisa and my mother around the farm on the golf cart, Doug insisted on coming along. He kept to himself the whole ride, but when we stopped and walked around, Doug stole glances at Lisa and laughed at everything she said, even when she was being serious.

When we were heading back to the house, I let my mother drive the little cart. She and Lisa sat up front, Doug and I in the back. When we rounded a curve along the cornfield, a strong wind blew Lisa's hair back in Doug's face. I looked over and saw him, grinning at the smell, eyes closed.

Doug looked at his face in the mirror and sighed.

"Doug," I said, snapping him back to reality, "she's thirty-seven."

At first he looked as if he were going to pretend like he didn't know what I was talking about, but instead he said, "I know it," then slumped his shoulders and walked out of the room. "Come on," he mumbled, "let's go eat."

Shelly, Fritz, and Doug sat at the dining room table with their backs to the stuffed marlin over the fireplace. Mike, Lisa, my mother, and Leah were crammed together on the other side. Joe and I sat at the heads of the table.

The windows were open, and fans were creating a constant breeze through the room. It had been in the upper nineties today, and the heat still lingered in the walls and rafters as night approached.

My mother had baked a ham with slices of pineapple and dots of cherries on its checked-grooved skin. I boiled a dozen ears of silver corn and made some scallop stew. Fritz sliced the ham and had everybody hold out their plates. Then we passed around the corn, potatoes, biscuits, and a little silver dish of cinnamon to be sprinkled on the pink ovals of meat. Mike, Lisa, Shelly, and my mother drank chilled red wine with orange slices floating in the red liquid. Fritz, Joe, and I drank the home-brewed beer. Doug and Leah had ginger ale.

The sound of talking and silver against china was like the whirring of a motor. The chandelier above the table spread strange shapes on the whiskey-colored walls.

Shelly was talking to my mother with half a new potato sprinkled with paprika stuck on her fork. She pointed the white ball at Leah and me. "I was the one who talked Fritz into getting these two together," she said, then looked back at him while he was talking to Doug (who was staring at Lisa and not paying attention) about how he used to collect robots when he was younger. "Can you believe Fritz wanted to set her up with a teen-aged mechanic he works with?"

Leah shook her head, cheeks glowing from embarrassment.

"I saw this boy only once—and he's the first person I've ever met who had fouler language than Fritz." She almost took a bite of the potato, then paused. "He even cussed when he was shaking my hand as we were introduced."

Leah smiled at my mother. "Shelly keeps my uncle grounded," she explained. "If it wasn't for her, God knows where that man would be now."

"Oh, he means well," Shelly said. "But half the things he does make sense only in his mind. He even wanted to set you up with some guy from my diner who's on parole." Shelly leaned over and patted Leah on the knee. "We had almost given up on trying to find you somebody until Tommy came along."

After that, my mom and Shelly exchanged stories about me as a kid. Leah listened and squeezed my knee when I tried to get them to stop. Then I looked around and listened to pieces of conversations. Mike and Lisa were talking about how long it had taken her to get here, and what routes she had driven. Doug and Fritz were going on and on about robots—but now they were talking about real-life robots the police use to dispose of bombs. Fritz was doing all the talking. Doug just nodded, eyes fixed on my brother's wife.

Lisa wore a sleeveless green T-shirt and white shorts. Her hair was curled and held back with a white headband. "So," she said, nodding to Mike and Fritz, "Tom tells me you two are brothers."

Mike looked down at his plate, and Fritz nodded weakly.

Lisa turned to Mike, who was examining his ham. "And you're Leah's father?"

He nodded quickly, then said, "Tom tells me your husband's a private contractor," with no real purpose or interest.

All week I had noticed that Fritz and Mike barely spoke to each other if Leah was in the room. If she was gone, they were chatty and friendly, but the second she appeared again, their conversation diminished to nods and grunts. Then one of them would walk out. Tonight, when we were all jammed together at the dinner table, Mike and Fritz had a hard time even looking at each other. It was as if there was a strange balance to their relationship with Leah, which secrecy kept stable. The funny thing was that everybody knew the truth. Leah had found out long ago that she had been adopted by Mike and his wife (who had refused our invitation because Fritz was going to be here). She knew that Fritz was her real father, and they, I was sure, suspected that this was something she had figured out. But not talking about it seemed to keep them happy. And they pressed on.

I sat back in my chair and folded my arms, listening to the voices muddle together in the warm glow of the room. Mike

relaxed and listened to Lisa go on about my brother's business;
Doug even mustered enough courage to join the conversation.
Shelly and Fritz were picking food off each other's plates, shiny-
faced from alcohol. And my mother and Leah made plans to
pick strawberries tomorrow morning while I was on the boat.

But I noticed one voice missing from the conversation. I
looked across the table at Joe. The candles in the centerpiece
blurred his face. He was sitting back in his chair, arms folded
just like mine, looking from person to person without saying a
word. I watched him over the blurring flame of the candles.
The talk became a low hum in the air. Joe looked up at the
ceiling and nodded his head as if someone were whispering plans
into his ear. Then his eyes scanned down the walls and onto the
carpet. His expression was bright as he looked at all the pol-
ished wood and the luster of his antiques. The marlin had been
dusted and its indigo hide shone like vinyl. The decoy ducks on
his fireplace mantle were in perfect formation. While looking
at the table a drunkard's careless smile cracked his leathery face.
Now that the dead-skin layer of dust and junk had been peeled,
the rooms were full of light, and Joe's house had come alive
with laughing voices. It had all come together for him.

ABOUT THE TIME I HAD PLANNED to take my brother out on the
boat, I was sitting alone on the dock. The heat of the boards
numbed the backs of my legs as I stared at the silvery surface of
the water, listening to the trees hiss in the wind. The water lapped
against the wall of cattails and grass around the dock, and bats
fluttered above me so dark I couldn't make out their shapes.

I heard the soft putter of an engine. I turned and saw a set
of headlights needle through the blackness. The Datsun came
down the path and stopped twenty feet away from the dock.
Dust swarmed in the long bars of the headlights, and the smell
of oil and gasoline gathered in the air. The engine died in a
raspy cough, and Leah stepped out, wearing a pair of jeans
shorts and a white tank top, a pink beach towel slung over her
left arm.

Leah and I came to the docks a lot on hot nights, to cool off
in the water. Then we'd drive back with the windows down,

feeling the rushing wind dry our skin.

"I've been looking for you," Leah said, bare feet sweeping on the dock. I felt the vibration of her steps clamber up my back. "Having a think?"

I nodded, then turned back to the oil-black water and stayed quiet. The night was filled with noise. Cicadas screamed in the trees around us, crickets sang to each other in bedspring chorus, and the dock lines on the crabbing boat cracked as they tightened.

Leah sat down next to me and hooked her arm under mine. I smiled at her, then looked down at my knees.

She nudged me with her hip. "You need to start telling me what's on your mind," she said. I didn't say anything, then she nudged me again.

"Why'd my brother have to not show up?" I slashed the air as if I were swatting a fly. "If there was one person I wanted to see this weekend, it was him."

"You never mention your brother, though. I didn't think you two were close."

"We're not," I said. "I was thinking we might *become* close."

Leah rubbed my arm. "I'm sorry."

"Goddamnit," I said, then plopped my head down on the heels of my palms. "We're not kids anymore—you'd think he'd give half a shit about me by now."

"Honey," Leah began, trying to calm me down, but I cut her off.

"I'm finally at a point in my life where I think me and my brother can get along. I mean, we both do contracting, he likes fishing, and we're *related*, for Christ's sake." I shook my head. "I just wanted to impress him finally."

Leah scooted forward and pitched herself into the water. Water flicked up into my face and shimmering rings marked where her body entered. A second later, she resurfaced and pushed her hair back out of her eyes. "Keep me company," she said.

"I don't feel like it," I said.

She blinked water out of her eyes. "I want to talk to you," she said, voice wavering from the effort of treading water. "Get in."

I climbed off the side of the dock and let myself fall into the water. Millions of bubbles like carbonation came into being down below and closed in on me. I swam forward and met Leah. I couldn't touch the muddy bottom. The gentle current of the water moved around us.

"I wouldn't try so hard to impress your brother," she said. "There's other people in the world who need you."

"I know," I said, feeling guilty.

"No. You don't." Leah tipped in the water and floated on her back, blinking up at the darkness.

"Who, then?"

Leah looked over, dipping in the mercury-like water. "His name is Robert Leonard Banner," she said. "You'll meet him in January."

I smiled and rocked backward so I too was facing the sky. The moon was like a white pebble dropped into a pool of tar. Its light shone grizzly on the treetops.

The water rushed around my ears and cut off all sound. I could only hear the pulsing of blood in my skull. Heat lightning sparked miles above me, purple-orange flashes behind a dirty veil of clouds.

Leah floated next to me, holding my hand. She stayed quiet, and I thought of all the people in Joe's house. I pictured them in the parlor. Joe would be sipping his beer, deep in thought in some corner. The lilting talk of Shelly, Lisa, and my mother murmured over the scratchy music of the record player, laughter from Doug and Mike and Fritz cracked any silence that thickened the atmosphere in the room. They would all talk with each other until sleep clamped down on them like a dizzying fog. Then in the morning they would greet each other as if they weren't strangers. I pictured them around the kitchen table, sleepy-eyed and anxious, wondering when Joe and I would return from work. For this, I couldn't stop smiling.

A cool wind picked up off the shore. The current rippled, then hooked around my arms and legs, dragging me away. My fingers pulled out of Leah's grip and my skin prickled from the cold. I looked over and saw her saying something to me, hand outstretched. But I could no longer hear. The water welled around my temples and around my face. My body felt heavy. I closed my eyes and breathed in the cool air. Then I let myself relax into the warm black water.